A Moment in

CONNEMARA

An Irish Love Story

A Moment in
CONNEMARA

An Irish Love Story

Annie Quinn

A Word with You Press®
Publishers and Purveyors of Fine Stories
802 South Tremont Street
Oceanside, CA 92054

ISBN 978-0-9884646-1-2

A Moment in Connemara: An Irish Love Story is published by:
A Word with You Press
802 South Tremont Street, Oceanside, California 92054

For information please direct emails to:
info@awordwithyoupress.com or visit our website:
www.awordwithyoupress.com

Cover design: Teri Rider, www.teririder.com
Book layout and typography: Teri Rider

Printed in the United States of America

For Noel

This story may seem like another Irish fairytale, but it's all true. I know because I lived it. It began in September of 1998 in a pub on Ireland's Connemara coast. Over the years, Noel Quinn, the man I noticed that night, smiling as he read a book in a corner of the room, never tired of telling people about how we met and the love affair that followed. After hearing our story, women would often ask me, "Now what was the name of that tour company? Where did you go in Ireland?"

Perhaps they hoped that they too might be love-struck by some Irish magic. The idea for this book was conceived from a comment Noel made years ago, when someone asked once again how we had met.

"Just read it in our book," he said.

"You've written a book?"

"Not yet," Noel replied, his blue eyes twinkling. "But some day."

Today is that some day. Here is our book, Noel.

Annie Quinn
Newport Beach, California
September 22, 2012

Enjoy the Moments!

Foreword

*W*ho has not been sideswiped at mid-life by unanticipated events, as Annie Quinn was? During the spring of 2010 Annie was grieving for the love of her life, Noel Quinn, who had died the year before. Wanting to set down her memories before they began to fade, she joined my memoir-writing class. As her love story came alive on the pages she read to us each week, the class urged her on. "Tell us more," we begged.

So Annie wrote—of the end of her first marriage of thirty years after her husband explained that there was someone else he wanted to marry; of the two women friends who insisted that she escape with them on a tour of Ireland; and of an evening spent in a pub on the Connemara coast, where she noticed a distinguished-looking man smiling as he read at a table for one. A widower named Noel Quinn. Our class, of course, was hooked.

When such upheavals happen to us, we tend to think that life will never be the same. What we fear, of course, is that we will never be happy or even at peace again. This book chases those fears into the shadows. As Clarissa Pinkola Estes writes in *The Gift of Story*, "The tales people tell one another weave a strong fabric that can warm the coldest emotional or spiritual nights. The stories that rise up out of a group become, over time, both extremely personal and quite eternal, for they take on a life of their own when told over and over again."

That is how I feel about Annie Quinn's book. Through it you will get to know two extraordinary people whose love for one another had a profound effect on dozens of friends and family around the world. Noel, who himself had seen hard times, had a joy for living that drew others to him. Although we never met, I came to feel as though I knew him. Sometimes I would run across a book or an idea, and think, *Oh, Noel would enjoy discussing that.* So this book reminds us to embrace happiness when it comes along, to laugh at the world's vagaries. From the night they met, that is how Annie and Noel lived. Even now Annie likes to close her notes and e-mails with, "Enjoy the moments."

I find it fitting that the Quinns' love affair began in Ireland, perhaps because I hold on to a lifelong belief in the leprechauns and fairies that populate the Irish countryside. Surely the little people played a part in this match.

Annie and Noel's story is a wondrous bit of Irish magic.

Jean Hastings Ardell

'I am of Ireland. And the Holy Land of Ireland.
And time runs on,'
Cried she. 'Come out of charity, come dance
with me in Ireland.'

—William Butler Yeats

Contents

A Moment in
CONNEMARA

An Irish Love Story

Beginnings

Serendipity

eptember 22, 1998. I was gone only ten minutes, just enough time for my universe to shift. I had just returned to my table in the hotel pub on the west coast of Ireland. A book now lay on the table, and I was surprised to see seated opposite me a distinguished looking man with salt and pepper hair, laughing eyes, and a quiet stillness.

"Hello," he said.

But wait, I'm getting ahead of the story. Let me go back a bit. My two best friends, Joan Bovard and Yvette Kilgore, and I were on a ten-day bus tour of Ireland. The trip had been originally planned by three of us couples to celebrate our fiftieth birthdays. But those plans changed when my marriage of thirty years suddenly ended. After my husband, Jim, announced that he wanted a divorce, Joan and Yvette changed our trip to Girls Only. We would meander the Irish countryside, laugh, relax, and enjoy the serenity of a land patchworked with forty shades of green.

Two days earlier, we had started out in Dublin and were now stopped for the night at the Connemara Coast Hotel, an old establishment overlooking tranquil Galway Bay. It was an ordinary Tuesday evening, when destiny and fate would intersect in my life. Our tour group had finished dinner, and several of us had continued our conversations in the hotel pub. When we entered, I had noticed a lone man reading a book in a corner of the bar. He was laughing, and I wondered what he was reading that caused him such joy. Joan ordered her favorite, Jameson Irish Whiskey, and Yvette and I ordered Irish coffees. With Irish music playing in the background, we chatted about the day's visits to Our Lady of Knock Basilica and the Connemara Marble Factory. Our animated conversation continued as we spoke of tomorrow's trip to the Cliffs of Moher and anticipated kissing the Blarney Stone. Joan expressed concern about the stone's germs and planned to wipe off the area with a cleaner before putting her lips on the cold, dirty stone. We found this hilarious and offered various scenarios, from whipping out Handi-wipes to coating Joan's lips with Vaseline. All the while, the man at the bar read his book and sipped his gin and tonic.

I felt stiff from sitting for so long and left to visit the loo. I adore flowers, so I revisited the lobby, which was filled with arrangements of lilies, stock, snapdragons, Gerbera daisies, and roses. The walnut furniture was upholstered in red velvet and gold brocade. Crystal chandeliers, spaced haphazardly around the room, reflected the feeling of dignified opulence in the gold-leafed mirrors on the walls. My ears strained to hear the classical music being played, which was overpowered by the merry chatter and native music emanating from the pub, which reminded me that I should return to the group. As I entered the room, I glanced at the table where the man had been reading his book. It was deserted.

While I was gone, a local had approached our group, saying he had overheard the conversation concerning germs on the Blarney Stone. Being from nearby Cork, he knew all the folklore and offered his expertise on Blarney Castle. Yvette had invited him to join us—and, as the gods or leprechauns ordained, there had been an empty chair across from mine.

"Hello," he said. "My name is Noel Quinn. I'm a widower. I live in Cork and am on a short holiday."

"My name is Annie. I am divorced and live in Orange County, California," I replied, and flippantly added, "It's much easier being a widower than a divorcee. After all, no one brings potato salad to a divorce."

To which he quietly responded, "You're the first divorced person I've ever met."

Noel had been married for twenty-five years to Mary McGrath. Within the first five years of their marriage, she developed multiple sclerosis and had been confined to a wheelchair during her last fifteen years. In February 1996, Mary had died of a brain aneurysm. They had been childless but cherished their many nieces and nephews. I explained that I had been married for thirty years and had three children, Heather, Jeff, and Wendy. We discussed traveling, politics, the ocean, our families, and music. Ah, the music. Noel spoke of his passion for the opera. My father loved opera; I remembered listening to that music as a girl. When I asked Noel which opera he would recommend for someone who was new to the form, he quickly answered: *La Boheme.*

Noel asked about the tour and what I expected to see in Ireland. As we spoke, the minutes slipped into hours. He laughed easily, and I loved listening to his Irish accent.

At some point, I reached for my Irish coffee and noticed a book on the table: *Neil Simon's Rewrites*: *A Memoir.* Only then did I realize that this was the man I had noticed earlier in the evening. I asked why the book made him laugh so. He enjoyed Neil Simon's work, he explained, and found the memoir so very funny.

Laughing at life—that's the key, I thought. I had found so little to laugh about in recent months. I asked to borrow the book for the night, promising to return it to the front desk early the next morning before our bus left. I offered to have everyone sign the book as a memento of our meeting in the pub. Noel thought that sounded great. I glanced at my watch, amazed to see that it was already morning—2:30 a.m. I thanked him for a wonderful chat, and turned to leave. "If I ever see *La Boheme*," I said, smiling, "I will think of you and this night in Connemara."

The Morning After

Echoes of "Good night, Noel" lingered in the hallway as Joan, Yvette, and I (the Neil Simon memoir in hand) strolled to our room. I threw my purse on my bed, sat down on the chair, and told the girls they needed to sign the book. Sleepily they agreed, and I watched as they wrote a quick note inside the front cover before slipping into bed.

But I was not at all tired. I had not been sleeping well over the past couple of months—too much turmoil to truly rest. My whole life had changed from that of being a wife of thirty years with a home to a divorcee very much in transition. Most nights, dreams of loss, shadows of grief, and the demons of fear awakened me after a couple of hours of sleep.

After getting ready for bed, I crept into the bathroom, where the light was still on, made a nest of towels on the floor, and opened the book. I was looking for the answer to a question raised that evening: Had Marsha Mason and Neil Simon ever married? I spent a couple of hours skimming the book, underlining funny passages and words that pertained to my chat with Noel. As I read, thoughts and images of the evening drifted through my mind. Our conversation had been so relaxed and comfortable, like speaking to an old friend. I had enjoyed our laughter and his stories. I finished perusing the memoir—I never did find the answer to my question, and added my brief note on the inside front cover of the book. My watch read 4:24 a.m.

When the alarm buzzed at six o'clock, we quickly showered and dressed, an amazing feat for three women sharing one bathroom. We finished packing—our suitcases were to be by the bus at seven o'clock so Jim, the tour bus driver, could load them before we left at 7:40. We had just enough time to grab a quick cup of coffee and a bowl of the wonderful Irish oatmeal. I left the Simon memoir at the front desk, explaining to the receptionist that Mr. Quinn would be picking up the book later that morning.

The large windows of the dining room faced Galway Bay, alive this morning with white caps, seagulls, fishing boats, and the famous Galway hookers, a traditional sailboat developed for the strong seas of the west coast of Ireland. The Galway hooker has a distinctive sail formation, consisting of a single mast with a main sail and two foresails. Traditionally, the boat is black (being coated in pitch) and the sails are a dark red-brown.

We found an empty table and quickly ordered. Suddenly Noel walked in and perused the room. His eyes stopped at our group, and Joan waved and invited him to join us. But as soon as he sat down, directly opposite me, Joan and Yvette stood up—it was like a teeter-totter effect: When he went down they went up. They said they had to go to the ladies room before our bus left. I was stunned that they left so abruptly—they had not finished their coffee or their breakfast. Noel and I made small talk, both saying how much we had enjoyed the evening. There was one quiet moment when our eyes locked, and I felt a connection to my very soul. Nervously I glanced at my watch. It was 7:35, time to go. I reminded him that his book was at the front desk, said good-bye, and hurried to the bus.

Joan and Yvette were on the bus, waiting. When I asked why they left the breakfast table, they replied that they thought Noel and I needed to be alone. Where had they got that silly idea? I wanted to know. They laughed and said it was obvious that we had connected. Apparently I had been too busy enjoying the moment to realize it.

As our bus pulled away, we saw Noel drive by in his black VW Golf on his way home to Cork. He had decided to leave early so he could visit with his brother in Shannon on the way. As the car drove out of sight, I was sure I would never see him again. We had not exchanged addresses, phone numbers, or given any indication that we would like to meet again.

The Bells of Shandon

September 25. Joan, Yvette, and I were enjoying an after-dinner chat in the mostly empty dining room of the Jury Hotel in Cork, debating what we should do for the rest of the evening. I glanced toward the entrance of the room as a solitary figure emerged from the shadows and casually walked toward us, as though we were expecting him.

"I came to show you my town," said Noel. "My car is outside."

We got up and followed him like the Pied Piper onto the busy sidewalk. Yvette ran back inside to tell one of our traveling companions that we were off to see the local sights with Noel, the man we met in Connemara.

A light mist fell as Noel drove the streets of Cork City. He was born and raised in an area of Cork called Gurranabraher and said that he loved showing people around his town. We drove through the narrow streets of Old City and the modern shopping center along the river Lee, passed by the Opera House and City Hall, then down Grand Parade, and up a steep hill to the Church of St. Anne's of Shandon. The bells were ringing as we pulled to the curb. Noel got out and I followed, unconcerned about the mist now falling. My friends, however, wanted to stay warm and dry in the car. Drawn to the pure tones of the chimes, I wanted to experience the character and charm of this sacred place, to feel the vibrations as the bells tolled.

"These are the famous bells of Shandon," Noel explained. "There's a song about them, which most Cork residents like to sing. It's a song of remembrance and nostalgia."

The mist grew heavier as the bells continued to peal in the quiet neighborhood, and I felt an intimate connection to this moment, this place.

"You girls missed an adventure," I said as I got into the front seat.

As we continued our tour, the girls kept asking to see Noel's home. I was surprised at their persistence. He finally agreed and we soon pulled into his driveway in the suburb of Douglas. This home was a typical Irish bungalow of concrete block with a tiled roof with a large picture window. We passed through the alcove that keeps out the dampness and cold, and sat in his living room, which was decorated in burgundy brocaded drapes, hardwood floors, and burgundy leather furniture. Noel disappeared for a bottle of wine.

Noel had never mentioned his occupation, and my friends were as curious as detectives. Yvette began to rummage through the magazines, mail, and papers on his coffee table in hopes of finding a clue. All she found were opera, travel, and music magazines, a few advertising circulars, and brown envelopes with his name and address printed. Yvette quickly sat back as she heard Noel in the hall. He poured each of us a glass of Chardonnay and sat down in his winged-back recliner.

The girls peppered Noel with questions about his occupation. His eyes twinkled as they kept guessing wrong—college professor, sales representative, accountant, banker. I sat silently, staring at him from across the room, and suddenly said, "I know what you do. You're a barber!"

He laughed. "You're right. How did you know?"

"I'm not really sure, other than I listened to a little voice of intuition."

We told Noel about our adventures since leaving Connemara. We had visited the Cliffs of Moher, the Ring of Kerry with its gorgeous ocean views, and Joan had survived kissing the Blarney Stone without being contaminated by germs. The Irish countryside was surreal, peaceful almost beyond description. Viewing the landscape from the bus allowed us to see a different view of the area. We could look over the tall hedges of fuchsia into the fields of various shades of green and brown.

"How did you find us tonight?" Yvette finally asked, knowing we had not shared our itinerary in Connemara.

Noel had asked various people in Cork which hotels had tours arriving on Friday night. The Jury Hotels were known for bus tours. There were two Jury Hotels in town, both, he learned, with a tour arriving that night. On Friday he called the hotels to ask if we were registered. The hotel did not have a record of my name, so Noel decided to choose one of the hotels and just show up. He had wandered through the lobby and pub before spying us in the dining room. The hour was growing late, so we finished our wine and began the drive through the silent sleepy streets to our hotel. Thanking him for his hospitality, we got out of the car and began to walk inside when Noel called my name.

"I have a gift for you, a remembrance of your trip to Ireland," he said, as he opened the glove compartment.

"This is my favorite CD of *La Boheme.* I want you to have it. One day I hope you'll see it in person."

I was flabbergasted. "Whenever I listen to this, I'll think of our chat in Connemara and the personal tour of Cork. Thank you so much!" I gave Noel a quick hug and turned to join my friends.

It was after midnight, but I decided to open the CD. A small piece of paper with Noel's name, address, and phone number was on top of the disc. I rummaged through my overnight bag for the box of note cards I had brought and wrote a quick thank-you. In the morning the Bells of Shandon were serenading Cork City as I dropped my note to Noel Quinn into the mailbox.

Pearl Avenue

*S*eptember 27. *Balboa Island, California.* I dragged my suitcase up the narrow stairs to my apartment on Pearl Avenue. I teetered on the small landing, searching for the new key zipped in one of the crevices of my overstuffed purse. I wiggled it into the new lock, pushed the door open, and stepped onto the new navy blue carpeting in my 500-square-foot sanctuary. I opened the door onto the upstairs patio, and a rush of sea air flowed through the cooped up rooms.

Home at last—or at least my new home on Balboa Island. With a suitcase filled with laundry and bags full of Irish souvenirs, maps, and books, I knew I should put things in order and prepare for my future. But I was overcome by the reality of my new life. I looked around the tiny place I had rented furnished. I had not had time before leaving for Ireland to put up pictures or knick-knacks. Now, weary from the long flight across the Atlantic, my mind drifted back over the whirlwind of the past few months.

I was in the midst of a divorce from the man I had begun dating when we were fifteen years old. We married at twenty-one, in December of our senior year of college, I at the University of Southern California and Jim at California State University, Fullerton. We had raised three wonderful children, two girls and a boy, and I thought we were living the perfect American dream, until I was blindsided by his infidelity. I had tried everything I knew to do to save our marriage, from pleading, changing, scheming, and crying, before accepting the reality that he was in love with someone else. I had kept my emotional rollercoaster a secret from everyone except my husband and my journal. I did not want to share our failures with others, believing that if our marriage could be saved it would be best if no one, even our twenty-something children, knew the truth of it all. I felt that people change their opinions of someone when they know the full situation. In fact, I was protecting my husband. I had been so focused on trying to fix my marriage, trying to manipulate events beyond my control, that I had been oblivious to the reality that my universe had shifted and my life had changed course. Looking back, I am not sure how I was able to survive the intensity of those days.

After we agreed to divorce, I met with my lawyer and family friend, Willard Reisz, to fill out the paperwork necessary to undo a marriage. Jim and I agreed to sell the house, split the assets, and get on with our lives. We put our home of twenty years, in Lake Forest, on the market. It had sold in late June, with close of escrow set for August 27. By midnight of August 30th we had to move everything out.

Weeks of sorting and packing had followed. I got boxes for each of the kids' pictures, artwork, school certificates, and trophies. I boxed up everything I thought I needed and piled up all the papers I thought necessary for business and taxes. I had to decide where each of our mementoes would go. I was unsure as to where I would be living, as I hadn't yet looked for a place to stay, so most of our possessions would go to storage. It was a sad time, yet somehow liberating. I had decided to let go of the past, as best I could, and float with the current instead of fighting a river or regret. Friends came to help me pack. Jeff came home for a short time before leaving for Nashville, Tennessee, where he was beginning a new job.

Everyone seemed to have an opinion about where I should live. My mother wanted me to move to Claremont because she felt I should be around family while I sorted out my life. She even offered to buy me a home, but I knew I couldn't move back to Claremont. Nor did I want to move to some non-descript apartment. I suppose I knew more about what did not feel right than what did. Then I remembered Balboa Island, where we had often vacationed when I was a girl and which held multitudes of wonderful memories. My family had rejected this idea: "What, are you crazy?...Why would you want to live there?...There's no parking...The rent is too expensive...You're not near any family!"

I decided to move to the Island.

I stopped in at the Balboa Island post office—zip code 92662—and rented a box. Jeff and I scoured the Island for a suitable rental for Bentley, my black toy poodle, Jason, my maroon-bellied Conure parrot, and myself. We read the rental cards posted on the bulletin boards along Marine Avenue and wrote down phone numbers to call. No luck. Undiscouraged, Jeff suggested we drive the streets to look for rental signs. We drove all twenty-two of the streets on the big and little islands. At 215 Pearl, we spotted a For

Rent sign. As we walked up to the bright blue Dutch door, a woman in her late seventies came from the recesses of the house. She had a small, furnished one bedroom, a bathroom with only a shower, a small kitchen and a door that opened onto a small rooftop patio over the garage. She did not accept any pets. Jeff explained that I was moving from Lake Forest, had gone through many changes to my life, and needed to keep Bentley. He wouldn't cause any problems, rarely barked, was housebroken, and only weighed seven pounds. She hesitated. We asked if we could see the place, but someone was renting it for the summer. We asked about the rent. I again asked about Bentley. Eventually she relented.

While I filled out the application, Jeff learned more about my future landlord. She and her husband had lived on the Island since the early 1950s. They had built the small apartment over their garage for income. They did not want any noise or problems from their tenants. They had raised two children here; one lived in the desert and the other inland, but neither liked the beach and rarely visited. After I got to know her, I would say her kids used their feelings about the beach as an excuse not to visit their mother. I handed her my application and a deposit. As Jeff and I drove away I was excited. Now I at least had a home and a place to send my mail, a place where I could begin again. And, with my Lifetime Elementary Teaching Credential, I could find work as a substitute.

In early August I was off on another adventure. Jeff was moving to a new apartment in Nashville, Tennessee, where he and his fiancée, Andrea, would settle after their marriage in March. He had sold his Jeep and purchased a new Honda, which he filled with his belongings. I would go along on the four-day road trip on Route 66. I have many fond memories of that trip, beginning with Jeff expertly avoiding a dangerous accident in the desert near Blythe, though it caused all four tires to go bald after he slammed on the brakes. (Luckily it was only the tires. Jeff thought he had damaged the car's alignment. We bought four new tires and set off again.) Driving through Arizona, we sang that dumb song by the Eagles, "Standing on a Corner in Winslow, Arizona." Along the way, we laughed, talked, and joked before pulling up to his new life. After helping him move in and buying a few essentials for the kitchen and living area, it was time to go. We hugged a little longer than usual at the Nashville airport. We knew both of our lives were shifting, though our love for one another would just grow deeper.

When I returned from Nashville, I felt as though my belongings had multiplied—so much to do before escrow closed. Each day brought challenges. Inspectors showed up, papers were signed, moving companies gave quotes, and I still was sorting everyone's stuff into the appropriate box or the trash. What a relief it would be to escape with Joan and Yvette to Ireland in September! The itinerary and airplane tickets had arrived, and whenever I could spare some time I devoured books and information on Ireland. Meanwhile, Jim and I signed the final paperwork for our divorce. I felt no regret, as I had tried everything possible to save my shattered marriage. Our divorce would be final on January 12, 1999. So I had a sense of inner peace, a feeling of optimism, and a budding curiosity about my future, at least some of the time.

Wendy's boyfriend, Andy, was turning twenty-one on August 24, and they invited me to join their celebration in Reno, Nevada. We stayed at Harrah's, where we gambled, dined, laughed, and sang a rousing "Happy Birthday" to Andy. The rest of the packing would get done somehow.

Escrow closed as scheduled on the 27th, and with it a huge weight lifted from my shoulders. Now we had until midnight of August 30th to clear out and clean the house. Eventually the boxes were all filled, stacked and sorted. Jim took his boxes away in a U-Haul trailer. The moving van took my boxes and the kids' prized possessions to our family storage unit in Upland—helpful, as it saved on storage rent. Wendy arrived from Northern California on the 29th to help with the last details.

Saturday seemed like the longest day of the year. As Wendy and I cleaned, we kept finding more items here and there. My car was packed to the brim with everything I was taking to Balboa Island. And then it was five minutes to midnight, and we were done. Still, we left a few things behind, like an old bicycle and an odd array of cleaning stuff we had no room for. Exhausted and with nowhere to go, since no hotel would take Bentley, we ended up sleeping on the floor of Jim's apartment in Dana Point. I slept fitfully waiting for the early morning light so we could leave for Northern California.

We drove to Rohnert Park, stopping along the way to let Bentley walk a little and to have lunch. We arrived early in the afternoon and unloaded some things from my car. We went out for dinner to a Mexican restaurant with Andy and his parents. While we were waiting for our food, Wendy handed me a present.

"Tomorrow is my birthday," I said. "Shouldn't I wait until then?"

"No. This is from Heather, Jeff, and me, and you need to open it now."

I opened the card and found out why. I was going on a hot air balloon ride in the morning. Hot air balloons had always fascinated me, and the kids thought it would be the perfect gift for someone turning fifty. Wendy was going with me and we had to be at the site at six o'clock, which meant awakening at four. I still cannot believe we were able to get up so early after the past few days of packing, cleaning, moving, and driving. That morning, the operator torched the fire to lift the balloon, set off a swoosh of heat and noise—and then we were sailing effortlessly over the Napa Valley vineyards. The ride was uplifting, no pun intended. It symbolized my newfound sense of adventure, a new decade of my life, and a small step toward my future.

On September seventh I moved into to my apartment on Pearl Avenue. Although she thought it was a terrible decision, Mom had insisted on helping. We met outside the apartment, and as I opened the door, she gasped. "You are not moving in here. This is ridiculous. It's too small," she commanded. "You're moving in with me."

"No, Mom, I am not moving in with you. I want to live here and be on the Island. I feel safe here. It will be fine."

"You just can't do this."

"I am doing this. If you want to help move my stuff in please stay. But if not, you can go home."

Mom seemed convinced that I had lost all rational thought. She could not seem to accept that my life had changed. I had always been the logical and responsible one in our family. Now I was unsure as to which direction I was headed. Mothers don't leave at a time like this, so together we moved my belongings into my Pearl Avenue apartment. I hung clothes in the one-door closet, folded lingerie for the three-drawer dresser, and stacked a few boxes of books, knick-knacks, and other treasures along the wall in the bedroom. I put a handmade quilt on the double bed and put my file box of important papers on the floor of the closet. After Mom and I had gone up and down those fifteen stairs a dozen or so times, my car was empty, and we were tired and hungry. Over lunch at Wilma's Patio on Marine Avenue, I tried to explain how I felt on the Island. I had only happy memories of this place and wanted to escape back into them.

I reminded Mom of a favorite story she liked to tell about my first vacation to the Island. She had moved my playpen, the old-fashioned kind with wooden rails, outside to the beach. On went my green checked floppy sunhat with "Annie" embroidered in red letters across the brim, zinc oxide dabbed quickly on my nose, and Sea & Ski suntan lotion rubbed up and down my squirming body. Mom put me on the playpen floor, which was cushioned by a beach towel. I looked around my new prison and saw my eight-year-old sister, Lynda, playing with her newfound friends, the boats in Newport Harbor, and the water lapping at the shore. I saw the gulls cruising above and felt the warmth of the summer sun. My eyes were drawn to the sand beyond the rails of my pen, and I crawled to the edge of the playpen. I thrust my chubby little hand through the rails and into the sand, reaching for the sparkly object that had caught my attention: a shell, my first gift from the sea, a tiny treasure with a lifetime of stories encrusted on its back. I picked it up and clumsily clutched it to my heart.

After lunch, Mom and I returned to our task. I had a mere nine days to get ready to leave for Ireland. I read and re-read the itinerary. Joan, Yvette, and I consulted on the phone for hours about what clothes we should take and how much money we needed. We decided that Ireland would be very cold so we packed silk underwear, wool jackets and pants, sweaters, and comfortable walking shoes. Remembering this makes me laugh, as Ireland turned out to be very warm, and we were not dressed correctly at all. Between the preparations, I walked the Island, feeling freedom and an unfamiliar sense of happy expectation. As the weight of the past few months fell away, I felt like I was seeing the world through different eyes. Pearl Avenue was the perfect place to renew my spirit.

A Shamrock on the Envelope

*I*t was autumn now, with Ireland a merry interlude between my past and the future. I was settling into my new life on Balboa Island. A couple of days a week, I worked as a substitute teacher for the Newport-Mesa and Irvine School Districts. On Wednesdays I worked with Mom in the Claremont offices of the family business, which entailed managing two shopping centers and maintaining seven town homes and an apartment building, spread out in several areas of Southern California. Helping to plan Jeff and Andrea's wedding, set for the following March in Sylacauga, Alabama, was a joy. There was the guest list to compile, and bridal showers, an engagement party in California, and the rehearsal dinner to organize. And I never tired of exploring the Island. I watched children digging in the sand, building their castles of dreams along the waters' edge, cheered for the fishermen on the public dock as they snagged a fish, and reveled in the salty air and sunshine.

October 10. It was time to sort the photos of Ireland for the scrapbook I planned to make. Sitting on my couch in my Pearl Avenue sanctuary, I thought of all the fun the three of us had in Ireland. The country does have a way of capturing your soul: the quilted landscape, all those shades of green, the hedges of fuchsia, the dramatic Cliffs at Moher, the jagged coastline, and the endless sea had mesmerized me. I loved meeting the Irish and felt so at home to their country. It is said that everyone wants to be Irish, and I believe it—I found the country magical. The nights in the pubs had been such fun, with the incessant Irish music that entertains the tourists but drives the locals crazy and the lively chatter that never seems to wane. Some day I hoped to return.

Arranging the pictures brought back memories of sights that I had already begun to fade. Here were Joan and Yvette kissing the Blarney Stone, upside down on their backs with their heads tilted backward. Here were a few pictures of our evenings with Noel Quinn in Connemara and Cork. I wrote brief descriptions of the places we had visited, so I would not forget them. After working for a couple of hours, it was time to for a break.

As I sauntered along South Bay Front, I watched the sailboats tacking endlessly down the bay, jockeying for position as they altered their courses with the light offshore wind. Three ferryboats were working, as the combination of sun and Saturday always brings the tourists to the beach. With no plan other than to get my mail, I decided to window shop along Marine Avenue, stopping in at the general store to see the new arrivals of toys and flags, pausing at Martha's Bookshop to see the latest releases, and visiting Dad's Donuts for a soft-serve chocolate and vanilla ice cream cone. At the post office I found a bill from the telephone company, a card from Yvette, *Westways* magazine, a few postcards with ads on them, oh, and a small white envelope bordered with green stripes, with two thirty-two punt (Irish currency) stamps depicting a robin. Postmarked October 4, 1998, Corcaigh.

"Who could this be from?" I said aloud to nobody.

I knew I could not wait until I got home to open this letter. I looked at the envelope again, but there was no return address on the front or back of it, and I didn't know where Corcaigh was. I slid open the seal and pulled out a one-page 5"x7" ecru note. I was astonished to read the following:

42 Clifton

Grange

Douglas

Cork

Ireland

Dear Annie,

The pleasure was all mine last week, but it's a pity our time together was so short. Anytime you want to come to Ireland just let me know, but in the mean time you can send your heart and soul over and I will take very good care of them. I got one of Buscaglia's books, living, loving, and learning, a friend of mine has a bookshop so he got it for me. My letter writing is a bit rusty. Tell me about yourself.

Take care

Love, Noel

P.S. Give my regards to Bentley.

Noel Quinn had responded to the thank-you note I had dropped in the mail before leaving Cork (or "Corcaigh" as it is known in Irish). Just as I had been taught, I had written my return address in the upper left corner of that envelope, and he had decided to write back. I re-read the note again and carefully put it back in the envelope. On the walk back to Pearl Avenue, I relived our brief time in Connemara and our nighttime tour of Cork City. I decided to answer his note, as it is always fun to have a pen pal in another country. I put on the *La Boheme* CD he had given me in Cork and pulled out a note card.

"Dear Noel," I began.

That letter was the first of many I would write over the next few months, as we became pen pals across the pond. We shared our interests, stories, thoughts, fears, and lives. I began to look forward to picking up my mail and often hurried to the post office to see if another note had arrived from Ireland. All through the fall and Christmas, Noel's letters arrived regularly; then, early in January, they stopped. I visited the post office daily expecting a letter and was disappointed when I found only letters and ads. Although it had been our routine to only reply to a letter received, I wrote again to ask if he was all right. Again, I heard nothing. I worried, but all I could do was wait. Finally, towards the end of January, I found a small envelope in my post office box.

Dear Annie,

I am so sorry you did not get the note I had my brother mail. I was in the hospital with a chest infection for two weeks. I am now recovering at my brother's house in Shannon. I will write when I return home next week.

Hope you are well,

Love,

Noel

I was very, very relieved to hear from him and realized how much I anticipated his letters. As promised, Noel sent a long letter the following week, and our commitment to being pen pals seemed to reach a new level.

Late one February evening in 1999, I was midway through writing a letter to Noel when a thought occurred: *Wouldn't it be fun to actually talk with him?* I found the original note that he had slipped into the *La Boheme* CD, and, before I lost my nerve, quickly called his number. As I heard the funny ring of the Irish phone, I almost hung up.

"Hello?" said his sleepy voice with an Irish lilt.

"Hi, Noel. This is Annie calling, from California. Were you asleep?"

"Annie! No, I just woke up. I don't work on Wednesdays, so I was just being lazy. Are you all right? Isn't it late at night in California?"

"I was answering your letter and just thought it would be fun to hear your voice and say 'Hi.' I hope I'm not bothering you."

"Bothering me?" I could practically see Noel's smile. "Not at all. I'm delighted." And so began our telephone conversations. Our letters still continued, though I did most of the writing, as Noel was more comfortable talking —he felt he didn't write well. But as our letters dwindled, our phone conversations only increased.

The Hospital at Coole

Although we lived six thousand miles apart, we spoke at least once and often two or three times daily, our conversations sometimes running for hours. Friends privy to this development sometimes asked what we found to talk about all that time. Well, we were catching up on each other's entire lifetimes—and oh, Noel's stories. They were endless, fascinating, and descriptive. One story was especially unforgettable. A few weeks into our telephone calls, we were chatting about our childhoods when Noel mentioned that he had been hospitalized for five years.

I thought I heard him wrong. "Five years? Why?"

He said nonchalantly, "Oh I jumped over a fence, and they thought I had broken my back."

"How old were you?"

"I was about three."

Oh my goodness, I couldn't even grasp this concept. A child in the hospital for five years beginning at age three. "Tell me again what happened."

"Oh, I was shadowing my older brothers, Mick and George, all around the fields. They were climbing under bushes, walking on walls, and jumping over the barbed wire fencing. Being show-offs and thrill seekers, my brothers decided to grab the barbed wire carefully and flip over the fence. Because I was too little, I didn't quite make the flip, tweaked my head and landed on my back. I screamed, my terrified brothers ran to get my Mum, and the neighbors all poured out of their terraced homes.

"Were you paralyzed? Did the doctor and ambulance come quickly?"

"Oh, no, I could move. Mum carried me home and the doctor was summoned. He found nothing wrong. But although I still played, sometimes when I bent my head I would get a sharp pain in my neck and back. The doctor, after eight months of watching my progress, suggested that I see the orthopedic doctor when he visited Cork."

Noel explained that there was only one orthopedic doctor in Ireland—yes, in all of Ireland. This was 1942 and the country was quite poor. The doctor practiced at an orthopedic hospital in the village of Coole, outside Dublin. He also traveled the country, examining patients

Noel had no recollection of his original visit with the specialist, testing, x-rays, or his diagnosis. All he knew was that the doctor told his parents that he should be hospitalized immediately as he probably had broken his back.

Noel proceeded with his story as casually as if he were talking about someone else. His Mum told him they were going on the train to Dublin. He was excited, as he had never been on a train. He and his Mum walked to the station in Cork City and boarded the large black train. He spoke of looking out the windows of the changing landscapes, seeing sheep and cows, and many streams and villages. In Dublin a car was waiting to pick them up. Again he was overjoyed, as he had never ridden in a car, as his parents, grandparents, and friends walked or bicycled everywhere.

The price of a car, let alone the price of petrol, was too much for his family. As he and his Mum got into the black shiny car he remembered a man and a woman sitting in the car, and the driver. As the adults chatted, Noel became mesmerized by all the people scurrying every which way, the buses, cars, and trucks moving in and out of traffic. Driving along the River Liffey, they came to a small bridge. He remembers the car stopping and his Mum jumped out.

"What do you mean, 'jumped out'?"

"Oh, they thought it was better for her to not go to the hospital with us. I felt so bad for my Mum as she had to leave me and go back to Cork alone."

"Felt bad for your Mum? What about you being left with strangers and driving to an unknown destination? You must have been terrified."

"I remember crying a bit, but it was for the best, and they were only doing what they thought was right."

I couldn't believe what I was hearing. A child left with people he did not know and his mother disappearing into the city of Dublin, and he was sorry for her?

"What happened next?" I asked, not sure I really wanted to know.

"Oh, they drove me to the hospital, where nuns wearing angel hats—they were the Sisters of Mercy—put me in bed. The nuns were caring, loving, and compassionate. The doctors and nurses tied me down."

This sounded medieval.

"They needed to keep me still, so they tied my legs and shoulders down and ran a strap across my belly. I could still lift my head, so they put a strap around my neck to keep it stationary. I could use my arms, but I could not sit up or lift my head."

"How often did you get out of bed?"

"Oh, never. I was in that position for five years."

I could not believe the conversation. I could not imagine leaving my child alone in the hospital for a moment, let alone years. "How often did your parents visit?"

"Only twice a year."

"Twice a year?"

"It was a long drive to the hospital, about five hours from Cork. My parents had no car or extra money for petrol. Twice a year my uncle's employer would kindly loan him his car, give him money for the petrol, and all my family would drive up for a visit.

"*Incredible, unfathomable,* I thought.

"What did you do all day?"

"We had school. We were given little slates and chalk to write, books to read, and the nuns would help us with our work. I do remember lots of laughter. We listened to the football and rugby matches on a small radio. On beautiful days they would wheel us outside—but only on good days without a hint of Irish mist, as it was too hard to push the cumbersome beds in the open dirt fields. They also kept the canvas sides rolled up during the day, so we could see outside."

"Canvas walls? What about in winter?"

"Oh," he said. "It was great fun, as snow would drift under our beds."

"It must have been so cold and damp."

"I don't remember that—we had blanket and pillows.

But the best part was all the other boys around me. We'd talk for hours, make up stories, and laugh a lot. I am not sure what was wrong with any of the other boys, but they, too, were confined to their beds. I also used my imagination and had great adventures all around the world."

I tried to get a clear picture of Noel's predicament. He was lying on his back, tied at his feet and neck and across his belly so he could not get up. He learned to read and did all of his school work lying on his back, took his First Communion lying on his back, ate all his meals lying on his back, and used bed pans. His parents visited twice a year. During one Christmas visit his parents gave him a stuffed black Scotty dog. The gift was taken away after they left.

"Weren't you sad?" I asked.

"Oh, no. I was OK, as no one else got a Christmas present, and I didn't want anyone to feel bad. I was lucky that my family were able to visit. Many of the other children never had a visitor. Anyway, I didn't need such stuff as we made up our own word games."

I was horrified to learn that Noel never had physical therapy and never got up for five years. I asked how they decided he had healed.

"I'm not really sure. One day the doctor came in and untied me. He did not do an X-ray or any tests that I remember. He just said, `You can get up.'"

"After five years! How could you walk with atrophied muscles?"

"Oh, I learned quickly." he said. "They told me if I could get to the little store at the end of the hospital ward I could have a candy bar." *Wow,* I thought, *a candy bar!* So I got down and grabbed on to the bed. I pulled myself along my bed and then grabbed onto the next bed. My arms were strong, as I did everything with them the last five years. I got to the end of the beds, with all the kids cheering me on, and crawled with my hands and arms."

"You must have been exhausted."

"Oh no, I was excited. I got the chocolate bar!"

"Did you have any therapy then?"

"Not that I remember. Within a few days, my parents came and we drove home to Cork."

"Just one day your parents arrive and take you home? I bet you were excited."

"I remember a bit of sadness leaving my friends, hugging the nuns, and saying good bye to my temporary family. But I was finally freed from the prison of my bed, happy to be outside in the fresh air, with blue sky, sunshine and lovely colors everywhere, unlike the canvas ceiling I had been looking at forever, and I was surrounded by my real family. I got to ride in a car for the second time in my life. And my Mum held me close the entire drive home."

"What did you do when you got back to Cork?"

"Oh, I don't know. Guess I just became part of the family. But I do remember my Mum treated me like a fragile piece of Waterford glass. She would not allow me to roughhouse or play on any teams, and my older brothers were told to protect me. I think my Mum was fearful that she would lose me to the hospital again."

"Did your back hurt any more?"

"No, it never hurt again. I didn't have any therapy or tests. After I got up, they all assumed I was cured of whatever had happened."

"Did you ever see any records of what the doctor had written about your condition or see any X-rays?"

"No. Years later I asked my Mum and Dad about the hospital stay and the medical records. They said they never had any. They had just done what the doctor had told them to do. They thought I would die if I had not gone to the hospital in Coole; they believed in the doctor. I honestly don't know to this day what was wrong with my back. I do know that my parents missed me and that my sister, Lilian, often caught Mum crying. It was such a sad time for Mum. And I have always felt bad that by being so far away I caused her sadness."

"Aren't you angry at all that you were tied down for five years? It has to make you mad or at least wonder, 'Why me?' Don't you feel like you missed childhood? Having children, I cannot imagine leaving my child for that long anywhere. I feel so sad for you and your Mum."

"I didn't miss my childhood. I had great fun. Four beds surrounded mine, at the head, foot, and either side. All the boys were funny. We used our imaginations and told great stories. My tongue was sharpened and the *craic*, as we say in Ireland, was mighty."

"The 'crack' was mighty? Sharpened your tongue? What does that mean?"

"*Craic* is news, gossip, and fun conversation," Noel explained. "It's a joy-filled experience with friends or family. Lots of laughter and stories told with wit. And 'a sharp tongue,' as we say in Ireland, is when someone has great storytelling ability and wit."

"Wow, you absolutely amaze me. You took a terribly bleak medieval situation and thought only of your Mum and family."

"Oh, it really wasn't that bad. The best treatment was given to me in the only orthopedic hospital in 1942 Ireland. I was lucky to get treated—and for free. It all worked out."

The story showed me Noel's compassion and patience, his absolute acceptance of life. This phone conversation in the spring of 1999 was the first of many times we talked about his hospital stay in Coole. Over the years I often seemed to drift back to the time and place of a little boy of three, excited about going with his Mum on his first train ride to Dublin and disappearing for five years into a strange hospital home of nuns with angel hats and canvas walls that rolled up; a little boy strapped to a bed and never getting up or sitting up; and having new "brothers" and friends. Each and every time I brought up his hospital stay Noel would say that it was not bad at all. And each time I would be amazed by his grace and forgiveness, his refusal of bitterness.

* * * * * *

During our telephone chats, I often gave Noel updates about my re-entry into teaching. In January of 1999, the Orange County Special Education System had assigned me to a class of fourth to sixth graders who had, for various reasons, been taken under the County's care. They were housed at the Albert Sitton Home, a converted convalescent home, with living quarters and two classrooms. The experience jolted me out of my own painful past. During my eight months there, I taught some ninety students who might be in my class for a day or for weeks. Oddly, I never knew what grade a child had been plucked from. I was given no history of these children, no files, no grades. I did not want the kids to feel they were simply repeating what they had previously learned, but tried to reinforce their skills. So I pretty much ran my classroom as a camp, where the kids learned about the artist of the week, did math speed tests, and read for fun. I also presented an author of the week, and taught creative writing.

On the day that Chrystal arrived, I was doing a silly unit on painting, using chocolate pudding as finger paint on the kids' desks. Messy, but it got them to smile and laugh. From the beginning, this girl intrigued me. Like so many of my students, she did not really like school and was suspicious of everything. But she had spunk and a love of learning that began to shine through. I had signed a pledge that I would not try to keep in touch with any of my students, but nine-year-old Chrystal touched my soul. I broke the rules, I confessed to Noel. I got involved. During my two months as Chrystal's teacher, I often kept her in the classroom for lunch and a chat, as I did with several other students, and so learned her story.

Chrystal had lived with an alcoholic mother in Fullerton. Through a neighbor, she had become acquainted with a thirty-something single woman named Teri Klein, who lived in nearby Anaheim. The neighbor told Chrystal that if she ever needed help, she should go to Teri's house. One day, Chrystal's mother went into a rage and kicked her daughter out of the house. Chrystal walked down Harbor Boulevard—so near Disneyland but so far from her reality, asked a stranger for money, and found a bus headed to Anaheim. Teri was at work, and as Chrystal waited for her on the porch, a concerned neighbor eventually called the police. The police picked up Chrystal just as Teri arrived home. With no custody rights, Teri could do nothing, but she determined to keep in touch. Chrystal was taken to Orangewood Children's Home, where abandoned and abused children go while the system determines what to do with them. The maximum stay is thirty days. Chrystal then wound up in the Albert Sitton Home and, consequently, my classroom there.

Teri quickly began a foster parenting course in hopes of someday making a home for Chrystal. And so began the painful court appearances and the push and pull between Chrystal's periodically repentant mother, Teri, and the child welfare system. And I stood by, feeling helpless, hoping that Chrystal's best interests would somehow prevail.

Noel Visits California

June 4, 1999. The International Terminal at Los Angeles International Airport was jammed with hordes of people awaiting flights from all over the world. I glanced up at the arrival board and read, "Aer Lingus Flight 144 from Dublin to LAX, arrival time 2:35 p.m., ON TIME." Another thirty-five minutes to wait. I paced the perimeter of the arrival area and tried to still my thumping heart. I wondered how I ever got to this moment. *Who am I really meeting? What am I expecting? What if I don't recognize him? What if it's a terrible visit? What if he isn't anything like our phone conversations and letters? Maybe Mom and my kids were right when they said, "What are you thinking, inviting a stranger you met in a pub to visit?"* My head swirled with negative thoughts and the noise of the overcrowded terminal. *Breathe,* I thought. *Breathe. Breathe in... breathe out.*

I called Yvette in North Carolina for reassurance. The phone rang twice before I heard Gary's voice, her husband and my dear friend. I explained that I was at LAX, nervous and scared, awaiting Noel's arrival.

Gary just laughed. "What are you worried about? You told me what a wonderful man Noel is. You've shared many of your conversations and letters with Yvette and me. Relax."

I chattered on, "But Gary, what if it doesn't work out? What if Mom is right? What if I don't recognize him? What if we don't have fun? What if this is all a *big* mistake? What do I do for three weeks with a man I don't really know?"

Again, I heard laughter on the other end of the line.

"Annie, relax, it will be fine. Yvette said he's a great guy—she liked him immediately. Show him around Southern California and treat him as you do all your visitors. Have some fun." After a pause, Gary continued. "Wish we lived closer so I could meet him. Maybe someday? Hey, remind me again what you two talk about on the phone for hours?"

Hearing those words thrust me back to reality. "Oh, Gary, thank you!"

"What for?"

"Just thanks for listening—you're such a great friend. Uh, oh, the plane has landed. Thanks again. Give my love to Yvette. Call you tomorrow."

I put on fresh lipstick and walked to the railing that overlooks the ramp of arriving international passengers. As my eyes searched each person walking up the ramp, I thought back over the nine months that had passed since we met at the Connemara Coast Hotel. My simple thank-you note had been written and answered, infinite cards and letters had been exchanged, and hours of phone calls logged between Southern California and Ireland.

I remembered the anxiety I felt in early March, when Noel had broached the idea of a visit to California.

"What?" I had tried to sound nonchalant.

"I just need to see you!"

'Oh," I responded softly. "When do you plan to do that?"

"I want to come at the end of May or beginning of June. I can stay about three weeks. Is that all right?"

"Yes, that would be great!" I said quickly, so he would not hear the hesitation in my voice. But his request put me off-kilter. My family had heard me talk about our correspondence and conversations but did not know the depth of our relationship. Nor did I, really. I wasn't at all sure how my three children and mother would respond to my gentleman caller.

As I often do when expecting visitors, I went in to tour guide mode, organizing an itinerary: We would visit the local sights—the San Juan Capistrano Mission and Orange County's beach towns from Newport to San Clement; then drive a long loop northward to visit the family cabin in Gull Lake in the High Sierras, Yosemite, the Napa Valley wine country, San Francisco, and Redwood City for the wedding of Heather's college roommate, Kris, where Noel could spend time with both of my daughters, before returning on scenic Highway 1 along the coast. My only regret was that Noel would be unable to meet Jeff, far away in Nashville.

That day in April seemed so long ago, and now Noel was here. As my eyes scanned the next group of arriving passengers I spotted a familiar face. He was walking up the ramp, pulling his black suitcase. He was dressed in a blue and white-checkered button-down collared shirt, Docker khakis, and comfortable walking shoes. He glanced up and when our eyes met, all my fears disappeared. I hurried to the entrance and hugged my Irish friend.

Everything seemed surreal as we drove the crowded airport ring road and entered the freeway.

"I bet you're tired after your long flight," I said, searching for conversation. "I still can't believe you're really here."

"I know," Noel replied in the lovely Irish accent I never tired of. "It doesn't seem real to be with you again. The trip was great and I slept a bit."

It was mid-afternoon, and the 405 Freeway was busy. Noel looked out the car window, and asked, "Where is everyone going?" He was amazed by the size of the cars, trucks, and motorcycles—much larger than in Ireland, where the petrol prices are higher and people are taxed on the size of their vehicle's engines. He noticed how stark and gray the concrete freeway was in contrast to the lush highways and country roads of Ireland. But the landscape changed as we proceeded down Jamboree Road and onto the Balboa Island bridge. Noel commented on the beachy island village, smiling as I showed him the post office where I visited daily, hoping to find a note from him. We pulled up to my newly rented cottage on Opal Avenue and stepped inside.

What a luxury it was to be able to talk with each other for as long as we wanted, and in the same time zone. I was excited to share California with him. Noel was fascinated by my collection of shells. Webster's New World Dictionary defines a collection: "To gather, to assemble, to accumulate." Well, I had done that, from Miami to Honolulu. My shells were arranged on my coffee table, strewn on my bookshelf, and surrounded a deep blue candle. A lone carved shell sat on my Gramma's antique round glass table. My shells filled empty cookie tins and collect dust in old woven baskets. Some were haphazardly thrown on the kitchen counter or sat in buckets, waiting to be washed and cared for.

Noel, I discovered, loved the ocean as much as I. We took to walking the beaches of Balboa Peninsula and Corona del Mar, feeling the salt spray on our faces as the waves crashed and the ocean came running toward us, like a long-lost friend. Noel found pleasure in helping me search the sands for the perfect shell, which I define as one without the scars and broken edges so common after a war with the ocean. "A perfect shell," I explained, "is a survivor of its turbulent life. I like to imagine the story behind the shell. Where did it come from? What became of the animal that lived in this small house? How far had the shell drifted until it landed on shore?"

"It is simply miraculous," I went on, "that some shells survive the trauma of their journeys. Abandoned by their animals to drift aimlessly on the ocean floor, swirling in currents, and often thrown to shore in violent turbulence, most shells end up in pieces that over time mingle with the sand. And yet some shells survive after traveling uncountable miles and land at the feet of hopeful beachcombers, like us."

When Joan and Ken came to dinner, they introduced him to margaritas, which he did not care for as he found them too sweet. Aside from the margaritas, it was the beginning of a delightful friendship. I was teaching for the County of Orange and sometimes had to work during Noel's visit. During the day, Noel would take Bentley for walks around the Island. Of course, my family was highly curious. Heather, who was working in Los Angeles on a documentary film about breast cancer and had an unpredictable schedule, suddenly phoned, wanting to know if she and her boyfriend, Derek, could meet us for dinner. My sister, Lynda, called: Could she meet Noel before we left for northern California? Everything happened so quickly, and given my apprehension about her disdain for my acquiring a gentleman caller, I chose not to include Mom in our dinner plans. (She expressed her upset over being left out). For some reason, which for the life of me I can't remember, we decided to meet at Dave & Buster's at The Block in Orange. Walking into the restaurant was a true American experience—I had forgotten that this was the adult version of Chucky E. Cheese's ("Where a kid can be a kid"). The lights were dim, the video games dinged, and music blared. Noel looked bewildered, and I was nervous about him meeting my family. Then Lynda and her husband came up, holding a fistful of tickets. They had been here for a while and were playing games. Noel asked what the tickets were for and they said they could win prizes. I still laugh at the craziness of this scenario, so different from Noel s usual pub or a quiet dinner. After Heather and Derek arrived, we all sat down in the dining room, which, fortunately, was quieter. An American menu can be overwhelming to a European, as there are so many choices and such large portions. I helped Noel sort out his order and then we got to know one another a bit. I thought it went well.

True to the itinerary I planned, we left Southern California's sprawling cities and drove north through the Mojave Desert on Highway 395. We stopped in Randsburg, a semi-ghost town, where we explored the old mines and sipped milkshakes at an old-fashioned soda fountain. At Twin Lakes in Mammoth, Noel was thrilled to see small pockets of snow in the shade. Just for the fun of it, he took off his shoes and socks and dipped his feet in the icy lake. We stayed the night at my family condo on Gull Lake. Luckily the Tioga Pass to Yosemite had just opened for the summer season, and we were able to continue the next day through the high country, across green meadows lush with wildflowers, and into Yosemite Valley, where the rivers and falls rushed with snowmelt. We had lunch on the patio of the grand old Ahwahnee Hotel.

We continued north to San Francisco, where I drove all over the hilly city. At one point Noel defended me by yelling out the window at a man who had shouted at me and made hand gestures in anger. I sheepishly laughed when I realized I was driving the wrong way down a one-way street. but Noel was my protector anyway. He loved the city's hills and vistas overlooking the bay, the Golden Gate Bridge, and Fisherman's Wharf. Before arriving at Wendy's in Rohnert Park, we drove through the wine country of Napa and Sonoma Valleys. It was fun to stop at some of the vineyards and see Noel's delight in the wine tastings.

When we arrived to pick up Wendy and Andy for the wedding, she was ready but told us that Andy had other plans and couldn't attend. So we three chatted all the way to St. Matthias Church in Redwood City. There, at Kris and Kirk Duncan's wedding, Noel felt right at home, as some of the guests were Irish, and he had great fun talking with them, and with Heather, Derek, and Wendy.

Noel loved seeing California's diverse landscapes

through my native's eyes. As we drove home along Highway 1, through Monterey, Carmel, and the rugged coast of Big Sur, so similar to Ireland, we talked and laughed. Somehow we never ran out of things to talk about, and I loved that I never had to hang up the telephone before a conversation was finished. As we experienced the grandeur of California, our friendship deepened and changed into something more, love.

Noel's trip was quickly coming to an end, however. He was to fly home in only a couple of days. We both dreaded the return to phone calls and spoke of various ideas of when we could see each other again. I spontaneously decided to book an airline ticket to Ireland in July.

A Fine Romance

Meeting Noel's Family

July 7, 1999. Tonight I met Noel's brother, Mick, and his family. The taxi picked us up, as no one drives after drinking in Ireland. I felt like a teenager again, about to meet the parents for the first time, my stomach full of butterflies as I clutched my carefully wrapped and beribboned hostess gift.

"Noel, tell me their names again?"

"My brother is Michael, but everyone calls him Mick. Therese is his wife. Stop worrying—they will love you."

"What are their kids' names again?"

"Graham is the oldest, Susan is his partner. Gary is married to Wendy—they were married last December. And they have a daughter, Gwen."

"Wow, all their names begin with G. Will they all be there?"

"Yes, I think so. They can hardly wait to meet you. I told them all about you.

Oh, my, I thought. *What are they expecting from this strange lady from America who met their little brother and Uncle Noel in a pub in Connemara?*

As the taxi pulled up in front of a house, I took a deep breath, grabbed Noel's hand, and climbed out.

"Relax, they will love you just as I do," he said. "And what does it matter if they don't? It doesn't matter at all between us. I love you. Just be yourself. They'll see."

I reluctantly walked to the door, Noel knocked. It seemed like an eternity before the door opened. And there was Therese, just as Noel described her, beautiful, blonde, petite, with an ethereal presence.

"Welcome to our home and to Ireland," Therese said. "Come in, come in. We are so excited you're here."

Mick was right behind Therese in the hallway. Noel hugged Therese, shook hands with Mick, and introduced me. It was funny to witness the handshake as Noel always hugged everyone, but Noel knew that Mick was not a hugger.

Their formal living room had navy blue carpeting, white furniture, with accents of gold. Mick offered drinks, and we made small talk. Therese spoke of the Fourth of July celebration they had celebrated a couple of days before. She thought it was great fun that Noel wore a "Happy Birthday America" T-shirt that he brought back from his visit to America in June. She also loved the star-shaped candles, Fourth of July napkins, and confetti I had sent Noel.

"Oh Therese," I said, realizing I still held her gift, "I brought you this small present."

She jumped up, disappeared into the other room, and returned with a festively wrapped present for me. We opened our gifts at the same time. Candlesticks! I had brought a pair candlesticks made by an American potter; Therese's candlesticks had a Gaelic design, made by a local potter. "Oh, Therese, I love them. My favorite color is blue and whenever I use them in America I will think of you."

I believe at that very moment Therese and I bonded. She had always been one of Noel's biggest cheerleaders, encouraging him to go out and get involved in life after

Mary died. Therese and I were similar in temperament and loved the same things. My fear of meeting the family was slowly dissipating.

"Why don't we go outside, as it's a lovely evening," Mick said. "We're going to have a barbecue."

The garden was softly lit by the candles Therese had placed all around. We sipped our drinks, chatted, and enjoyed the balmy evening as one by one, the rest of the family arrived. Graham and Susan first, then Gary and Wendy, along with their friend Sinnead. Kevin, an American who had gone to school in Dublin with Gary, arrived next. Then Gwen rushed in, just back from her flight. (She is a stewardess on Aer Lingus). Each greeted their Uncle Noel with a warm embrace, and I could see the love they felt for him.

We sat around the large round patio table, Noel beside me, as I got to know his family. Therese had set the table with her finest china and silver wine goblets. The starter, which we call the appetizer, was Irish salmon and buttered brown bread. Wine, a choice of red or white, was poured in to our goblets. When the steaks were ready, Therese brought out fresh steamed broccoli, cauliflower, carrots, roasted potatoes, and mashed potatoes.

The candles gave a magical quality to the evening, and I kept squeezing Noel's hand, making sure this was not all a fantasy. Noel's family was welcoming me to their world. They shared stories about him. His nieces and nephews spoke of how their uncle encouraged their achievements and loved being with them. The wine flowed, the candles flickered, and overhead the stars shone. Then the party pieces began, a marvelous Irish custom. Each person performs a favorite song, poem, limerick, or recitation, unaccompanied by music. I had never seen anything like it. Everyone had his or her special song. Mick's specialty was Frank Sinatra. He liked to sing "Young at Heart" and "Fairytales May Come True," and, in my opinion, was a better singer and a wiser man than Frank. Therese did a rendition of "If I was a Lady," a wonderful poem she recited with a scarf swirled 'round her head. And Noel sang "Summertime" from the depths of his soul. We continued into the night, singing Irish ballads, popular songs, and did a bit of Irish dancing. And always the stories and the humor—so this was *craic*! Noel was right. Therese and Mick and their family were gracious and loving.

During that hectic first week of my visit I became ill. Noel made an appointment with his doctor, Maura Cohr, and brought me to her office, called "the surgery." Dr. Cohr examined me, wrote a prescription, and said I should feel better in the next few days. I was a bit nervous meeting her as she and Mary had been close friends; Mary, in fact, had been the nurse to Maura's father, also a doctor. Maura wanted to know how Noel and I met, and I told her the whole story. She shared memories of Noel and Mary and talked about her life as a family doctor in Ireland. Maura wanted me to meet her husband, Don, before I went home. I left her surgery feeling as though I had found another Irish friend.

"Are you all right?" Noel asked anxiously as I returned to the crowded waiting room. "Annie, tell me why was your appointment so long."

"Oh, we were just talking about how I met you, our time in America, and what I thought of Ireland. Why?"

"I was worried. No one usually spends that much time with the doctor. I thought something was wrong, and her waiting room kept filling up with patients," Noel said, shaking his head.

Later that week we met Don and Maura Kelly at the Roachestown Park Hotel bar for a drink and a chat. Don was charming and we had a wonderful, though brief, visit. They had us promise that the next time I was in Ireland we would come to their house for dinner, and Don would cook.

Two days later Noel and I drove to Shannon to meet his other brother, George, and his wife Kay. As we drove north from Cork, we once again got lost in conversation about the passing countryside of ruins, side roads, and villages. Noel was showing me his Ireland as I had shown him my California. I was just grateful that he drove, as I was uncomfortable driving on the Irish side of the road. But as we parked behind George and Kay's home, I got nervous all over again. Once again, Noel was reassuring as he walked me across the narrow street, unlatched their back wooden gate, and escorted me through the garden. "George, Kay!" he called out, as we entered their kitchen. George was about 5'5", with salt and pepper hair and clear blue eyes. He was a hugger, and as I stepped up into their kitchen, he said, "Welcome, Annie. Wow, you are tall!"

Kay was about 5'3", with golden brown hair, twinkling eyes, and a great smile. She immediately offered me a cup of tea. I told her how happy I was that Noel had been able to recuperate from his chest infection at their home. "He said you took great care of him."

A little girl appeared, adorable and very shy. Kay introduced me to their granddaughter, Haley. She was three years old and stayed with Kay when their daughter, Maria, worked. Over biscuits and tea and coffee at the table, Noel told them about his trip to America, and I told them how much I loved Ireland. They asked about my family and life in American, and I told them about my kids. We also told the story, again, of how we met in the pub in Connemara. The time flew by and then Maria arrived. She was a tall, beautiful girl with long black hair. She hugged her Uncle Noel, who was also her godfather, and grasped my hand in friendship. She sat down at the table and joined our conversation. Then Pamela, their other beautiful, tall, longhaired daughter, and Phillip, their son, and his wife Ruth, arrived to meet the lady from America. Maria told us about her son, Jake, who was at school, and Phillip and Ruth shared stories about their two daughters and two sons. Maria and Haley were going for a short walk and asked me to join them. We walked down the street and across the pathway to the corner store to buy Haley a lolly (popsicle). Maria asked about Noel and our meeting, and then asked what was becoming a perennial questions. "What do you talk about during all your phone conversations? Don't you run out of things to say?"

"Oh, no, we never run out of conversation. We have so much to learn about each other, from our upbringing to our families, from our interests in music, books, and movies, places of travel and our dreams for the future. We never seem to have enough time to talk and never run out of things to talk about."

Maria looked like she still couldn't fathom talking for hours.

The afternoon faded into early evening, and we bade our good-byes with promises to meet again soon. They walked us to the car and gave us both a hug. As we drove away, I told Noel how welcomed I felt. Noel was right. Everyone was so hospitable and friendly, and I clearly saw how much they all loved and respected their Uncle Noel, an important part of their lives.

At the end of the week, we visited Noel's sister, Lilian, and her husband Jerry, for tea at their home in Cork. As we pulled up to their bungalow, I was nervous all over again, but once again, received a warm Irish welcome. Lilian, a tiny woman with short-cropped brown hair, large blue eyes, and deeply tanned skin, served tea, coffee, and various biscuits in the living room. She and Jerry have seven children and we spoke of each of them. They also told us about their trips to the Canary Islands, where they rent an apartment for a couple of months each year. They love to ballroom dance and also travel extensively throughout Ireland in their motor home. Wherever there is water and a bit of sun they will stay. They asked about America and told me they had visited New York City for a short time. The afternoon slid by and then we bade our farewell as we had a dinner engagement. I told Noel how much I appreciated meeting his brothers and sister. They had given me a better understanding of him and his role as the protected baby brother of the family. He looked at me and just laughed.

That night we visited Ann and Bob Warren for dinner. Like Noel's sister-in-law, Therese, Ann is among those who take credit for Noel's trip to Connemara, as she, too, encouraged him to get out of the house and meet people. I do think both of these women had no idea when they urged Noel to go on a weekend trip that he would meet an American woman who would completely change his world. The Warrens had been friends of Noel and Mary for many years. Ann and Mary had gone to nursing school together. I was nervous about meeting them for the first time, too, but that was foolish, as they were warm, gracious and so hospitable. Their home was lovely as was their garden, which I mistakenly called a "yard." Bob quickly corrected me—a yard in Ireland is like a car yard. As I was saying, their garden was magnificent. The Warrens had moved into their home almost thirty years ago and Bob planned and planted the entire garden. Now towering trees shaded the well-cultivated flowerbeds that bordered the emerald lawn. Gin and tonics were served on the patio. We still joke about their "yard," but the time they must spend to make the garden look as it does is truly amazing. Throughout the evening, we talked, laughed, and got to know one another. I learned that they had three children; in fact, their son, Mark, is Noel's godson. We promised to keep in touch, and as we drove away I felt I had found new friends.

In 1999, I also met Denise and Sean McGrath, Mary's sister-in-law and brother. Noel and I had been exploring the countryside of County Cork and ended up in Ballycotton, a picturesque fishing village on Ireland's southeast coast where McGrath's Pub is located. The McGraths had been wonderful to Noel, continuing to invite him to family events and dinner, after Mary passed away. We stopped in at the pub, where Denise greeted me with open arms and Sean offered a cautious "hello." As we sat on barstools, they shared family history and stories of Noel with me. Denise and Sean had six grown children. As a girl, their daughter, Susan, had always wanted to marry her Uncle Noel when she grew up. Sean had two brothers living nearby, Phil in Ballyrobin and Michael in Ballyadreen, where their Mum, May McGrath still lived in the family home. Sean's sister, Dymphna, lived in England, as did his other brother, Father Tom, a priest. And his other sister, Betty, known as Sister Eilish, was the principal of Sacred Heart Secondary School in nearby Clonakilty.

Betty extended more Irish hospitality to Noel and me with an invitation to lunch in Clonakilty, which was celebrating its award as Ireland's Tidy Town of 1999. The term "Tidy Town" refers to a national competition, held since 1958, to recognize notably beautiful towns. With its brightly painted shops and lush hanging floral baskets over the storefronts, Clonakilty qualified. After a mix-up as to which restaurant we were to meet at, Noel and I found Betty. Over lunch, she shared her love for Noel and told of his years with Mary. That afternoon was the beginning of another wonderful Irish friendship.

Planning for Noel's Sixtieth

September 1999. Noel's big birthday was on the horizon. He would turn sixty on December thirteenth. He deserved a wonderful, fun-filled birthday, and I determined to find the perfect gift. But what should I get? One afternoon, as I was listening to the *La Boheme* CD Noel had given to me, it came to me. Maybe we could see *La Boheme* at the Metropolitan Opera in New York City. I had once asked Noel what his dream wish would be. He responded that he would like to see an opera both at the Met in New York City and at La Scala in Italy. Maybe, just maybe, I could grant the first part of his wish. I hurried to the computer and checked the Met's web site to see if that was possible. On the Met's calendar for the 2000 season, there it was: *La Boheme* would be performed in April. Wow. I called the ticket office and booked two tickets in the orchestra section for Wednesday evening, April 19, 2000.

Now I needed to plan the rest of Noel's birthday celebration. After much thought, I decided that we could meet in Charlotte, North Carolina, for a visit with Gary and Yvette for a couple of days. From there, going by train to New York City might be fun. Noel could see more of

America as we traveled north up the Atlantic coast until we reached Grand Central Station. I went online and booked reservations at a hotel near Rockefeller Center.

By the end of September, the plan was complete, and I decided to start his celebration early. Almost daily I mailed a postcard or letter about his upcoming birthday. He was filled with curiosity. In November I mailed a singing birthday card that held two tickets for *La Boheme*. On the outside of the envelope I wrote, "Do not open until December 13, 1999." He promised to *not* open it.

I had asked him not to open the card until I called that day. On the thirteenth of December, my phone call woke him up. After singing "Happy Birthday," I said he could now open the card. I listened through the phone as he ripped open the envelope. I could hear Hoops and YoYo, Noel's favorite Hallmark characters, singing in their funny voices. When the song ended I heard silence, then a gasp.

Noel's teary voice finally said, "Annie, really?"

"Yes! Happy, happy sixtieth! I'm so excited, as we'll get to see *La Boheme* together."

"I can't believe this. Wow!"

As I filled him in on the rest of the plans, Noel grew quiet. When I got to the end, he simply said, "I'm speechless."

After we got off the phone, I realized that Noel was overwhelmed. I loved hearing the disbelief in his voice and the childlike wonder of his thank you. I felt like a fairy godmother that had come down, waved her magic wand, and given him the perfect unexpected gift. I couldn't wait for April.

Christmas in America

*D*ecember 1999. As I reflect on Noel's first Christmas in America and the events that followed, I am again reminded of all that changed in a short time. But at the time, I had simply lived day by day, not realizing the intensity of those months.

Noel arrived the week before Christmas to spend a couple of months with me on the Island. I was excited to see him but apprehensive about his first meeting with my parents and his presence at our traditional Christmas Eve celebration, where he might be devoured by so much family.

Noel finally met my mother over lunch after our usual family business meeting. We went to an Italian restaurant, Pizza & Stuff, where Mom was cordial, cold, and awkward as she quizzed him about his background and his work. She expressed surprise that he had left his business (even though it was in the capable hands of a friend) for a two-month vacation and surprise that he was interested in me. When the waitress appeared to take our order, Mom was surprised that Noel ordered a glass of wine, forgetting that he was, after all, on vacation. She disapproved of our meeting in a hotel bar, even though, as Noel always said, it was a five-star hotel pub, not a sleazy pick-up bar. Noel took it all in stride. At the end of the meal, the waitress placed the check on the table. Now, as anyone who ever knew my mother could testify, she always picked up the check, especially for a Christmas business luncheon; but this one she did not touch. Noel casually picked it up, asked me how much to tip the waitress, and paid for the meal. After we said our farewells, I breathed with relief that the dreaded meeting was over. I explained to Noel that Mom had shown her disdain of our relationship by not picking up the bill.

Being Noel, he just laughed, and said, "Give her time, Annie. My first mother-in-law didn't like me at first either, and we are now great friends."

The next few days flew by. As we walked the Island at night, we took in the holiday decorations on the bay front homes and the Newport Harbor Boat Parade, with its boats ablaze in lights and color. Wendy arrived from Northern California, and she and Heather drove down to say hello. On Christmas Eve, we all gathered at my parents' home. Our family kept the tradition of Santa Claus, exchanging our presents on Christmas Eve, followed by a light buffet. As our children grew up, each one began their own tradition on Christmas Day.

This year the holidays seemed especially difficult, given Dad's fragile health. He had not been well since his aneurysm two years earlier. Now he slept great portions of the day, seemed a bit confused, and had lost his wonderful sense of humor. When we arrived, he was sitting in the family room. I gave him a kiss on the cheek, and said, "Dad, I want you to meet someone. This is Noel. He's visiting me from Ireland."

Dad looked up with a blank stare and shifted his eyes to Noel. He grasped Noel's hand, and said, "Hi." Nothing else, just, "Hi." I could see in the confusion in his eyes. I don't think he remembered Jim and I had divorced earlier in the year.

Noel said, "It's nice to finally meet you. Annie has told me so much about you."

Again, Dad's blank stare. I was saddened by that moment, as I wished Noel could have met the father I remembered as a child, not this shell of a man. Dad had always been my hero. He was 6'3", tanned and athletic. He was always getting my sister and me in trouble with Mom by playing games at the table, making us laugh when we shouldn't, buying junk food for my friends and me, and taking us on day trips to Corona del Mar. He was my swim coach when I trained for the Junior Olympics, oh, so long ago. But the moment continued, as Noel did not let go of my father's hand, as if to continue their connection. I guess Noel was silently telling Dad, through touch and eye contact, that he was here to take good care of his daughter.

The Christmas Eve merriment continued as my aunt, uncle, and cousins arrived. Then Heather and Wendy arrived, followed by my sister, Lynda, and her family. Everyone loved Noel's Irish accent. The kids ran around, so excited for Santa Claus, the noise of the room increased, and Dad became agitated. He needed quiet and wanted his routine restored. Linda, the caregiver Mom had hired, helped him off to bed.

Noel found the artificial tree and the piles of gifts amazing. I had never looked at our tradition through another's eyes and realized how overwhelming it must be. As a child he remembered receiving one gift, such as a toy car. If they were lucky they might also get a fresh orange. During his marriage, he and Mary spent Christmas at a local hotel, where her wheel chair could be accommodated. They would arrive Christmas Eve afternoon and dine alone. Family would come by on Christmas Day for a celebration drink.

Noel had bought my mother a gift from Ireland. He had fussed over the choice, spending hours looking for the perfect gift before deciding on an Irish linen tablecloth. I think Mom was a bit surprised by his gift, and although she thanked him, she did not let down her guard. Yet to my surprise she had bought a gift for Noel, a pair of binoculars.

On Christmas morning we attended Mass at St. John Vianney Chapel on the Island, then stopped by Betty Dooley's home on Balboa Peninsula for coffee. Betty was one of Mom's dearest friends and had known me since I was two years old. Later in the day we drove up to my sister's home for Christmas dinner and another round of family. Wendy left early to spend a bit of Christmas with her boyfriend Andy; and we drove home, completely exhausted.

We were watching a Christmas show on television when the phone rang.

"Hi, Mom," Wendy gushed. "I'm engaged! Andy and I were giving each other our Christmas presents, and then he asked me to marry him. The ring belonged to his Great Aunt Hilary. I'm engaged!"

"Oh, Wendy, I'm so happy for you. Tell Andy congratulations. What wonderful news!" As she hung up, I realized we were embarking on yet another adventure.

* * * * *

New Year's Eve was unique: a new millennium and the first New Year's Noel and I would spend together. The media had made much ado about the possibility of computers crashing and banking being disrupted. Some people even thought it would be the end of the world. I was never much for New Year's Eve and Noel felt the same. We stayed home for a dinner of perfectly barbecued steak, steamed broccoli, salad, and, of course, Noel's baked potato. We enjoyed the intimacy of our home-cooked meal, candles, wine and one another's company. Afterwards we strolled hand in hand around the Island, stopping just before midnight to sit on a bench to watch the explosion of fireworks. As we kissed at midnight, I was filled with anticipation for the year ahead. Noel and I would meet in April to celebrate his birthday; we would travel to Scotland, Ireland, and Wales with the Bovards and Kilgores in September, and I was now flung into plans for Wendy's wedding in July.

Thirty Days and a Bit

*I*n the middle of January, my father's body began to give out. He had endured heart problems, by-pass surgery, a pacemaker, poor circulation, and a stomach aneurysm. After each of these medical events, a bit more of his spirit seemed to wane. He spent most of his hours in the hospital bed Mom had ordered for home. After his aneurysm in 1998, Mom and I had met with a Presbyterian grief minister, who described the dying process: Death, like birth, basically follows the same process, only in reverse and down an invisible "death" canal. Both the baby and the dying person travel this journey alone, though surrounded by loved ones. It is a mystery, timed to each unique individual.

Dad grew worse. Wendy flew down; school wasn't beginning until the end of the month. To divert our sadness, we made time to shop for a wedding dress and looked at venues. Late one afternoon, Wendy put on my old wedding dress and long cathedral train, and visited Dad's dimmed room. "Hi, Grandpa," she said.

Although he did not respond, his eyes never left this white vision, veil trailing, as she circled the room. I always wondered what he was thinking as his radiant granddaughter drifted through his room.

The family continued to flow in and out of the house as Dad slipped further from us each day. I often sat by his bed, holding his hand. Since Mom had not called in hospice, he was eventually taken to Pomona Valley Hospital for care. He fell into a deep relaxed sleep, his breathing more shallow with each intake. For what I knew were his last hours, Noel and I stayed late, he on one side of the bed and I on the other. Finally Noel held Dad's hand and said a silent prayer and we decided to return the next morning. Dad took his final breath, however, very early in the morning of January 25.

The funeral was held two days later. Jeff and Andrea flew out from Nashville, and I was glad that my son and his wife would finally meet Noel. They liked each other immediately and went on various errands, which gave them time to chat and get to know each other, while I helped organize the reception at the house. The funeral was full of Dad's favorite memories, pictures, and music. Everyone contributed to the eulogy. The great-grandchildren shared the fun of Grandpa acting like a monster and scaring them. Listening to the stories, Noel was able to visualize something of the man Dad had been, husband, father, grandpa, uncle, coach, teacher, fisherman, sailor, painter, former professional football player, and horseracing aficionado.

After the service, everyone went back to Mom's house. I was talking with my ex-husband, Jim, in a room off the living room when Noel walked in with a bag of trash looking for the way to the garage, which now seems rather funny. We were all a bit startled.

"Noel, this is Jim; Jim, this is Noel," I said.

Noel put down the trash and extended his hand. Jim grasped his hand, and they both said, "Nice to meet you."

Awkward small talk continued until Noel excused himself, and with directions from me, scurried off to the garage. I quickly finished my conversation with Jim and went to find Noel.

Five days after Dad's funeral, Noel's time was up and he had to fly back to Ireland. As happy as I had been to drive to LAX in December, I was sad to return there in February. Noel checked in at the Aer Lingus counter, where the attendant checked his passport, and asked all the silly questions about his baggage. (Really, is anyone going to say, "Yes, someone else packed my bag." Or, "Yes, the bag has been out of my sight for most of the morning." Or better yet, "Yes I have packed a gun and explosives. Just want to let everyone know, as one thing I am not is a liar.")

We had a little over an hour to hang out. Each time this hour seemed sadder and more difficult. We dreaded these last moments in the airport. We would linger over lunch, continuing our conversations about anything and everything. I again told him how wonderful it had been that he had been with me over the last couple of months. I don't think I could have gotten through losing Dad without Noel beside me, holding my hand, sharing words of comfort, or just sitting in absolute stillness in the moment. Noel and I shared one last kiss before he joined the line for security. He gave me one last look, a slight wave, and disappeared behind the security screen.

I drove home alone with my thoughts, missing Noel already. Although we still wrote and spoke on the phone for hours, our times apart seemed endless. The three-month visitor pass to America was silly but would continue unless we married. Suddenly I realized that out of habit I was driving in the carpool lane. I laughed and then faced the dilemma of crossing over the solid line, which could mean a fine, or remaining in the lane until it was safe to exit, which could also result in a fine, as I had no passenger. Noel and I often laughed about his role in the car as we traversed the freeways; he was my dummy, allowing access to the carpool lane.

The next few months seemed to crawl by, though I was deep in wedding plans, helping Mom settle Dad's estate, and working in the family business. Wendy chose the historic Balboa Pavilion for their wedding and reception, just a ferryboat ride away for me. Steven Metcalf, who had been the youth minister at our Presbyterian church in Lake Forest, would perform the wedding. The menu was planned, the DJ booked, a photographer chosen. Wendy purchased her wedding dress (which turned out to be one of the first dresses she tried on in January), and the bridesmaids' dresses were ordered, and the rose centerpieces selected. So much to do in a short time, but manageable, even with Wendy away at Sonoma State University. Since Mom had been so busy with Dad in December and January, I had become more involved in the day to day the business. I often drove to Mission Hills, in the San Fernando Valley (mindful of inadvertently drifting into the carpool lane) to our shopping center to meet with tenants, walk the property, and troubleshoot any problems that might occur. Luckily we could rely upon a wonderful man, Mike Brenna, who tried to stay one step ahead of the maintenance needs and tenants' questions.

La Boheme: A Dream Come True

*I*n April, Noel and I met as planned in North Carolina to spend a couple of days with Gary and Yvette before boarding the Amtrak in Charlotte. Once on the train, we stowed our suitcases, and sat down in our seats. We did not have a compartment, as it was only a long day's journey to New York City. As the train sped along, we were lost in the clickity clack of the rails. The scenery, though, was a disappointment, as most of what we saw from the train was the backyards of homes and businesses and often-rundown areas. We stopped in Washington D.C. just long enough to disembark and breathe in the fresh air. When we pulled into Grand Central Station, it was even more vast and alive than I had seen in the movies. The hustle of people, trains departing, and loudspeakers blaring took our breath away. As we rolled our luggage outdoors toward the taxi stand, I thought, *We're actually here, in New York City, together. Another adventure has begun.*

In the back seat of the taxi we took in the city's bustle of nightlife. After we checked into the Hilton New York Hotel on the Avenue of the Americas, we went to find a restaurant. Noel had been here the year before for a whirlwind tour centered on St. Patrick's Day. I had visited

New York a couple of times but did not recall the same sense of excitement as I now had with Noel. We spotted Rosie O'Grady's Irish Pub near our hotel and went right in. We felt right at home since the staff was mostly Irish, and, as Noel would say, the *craic* was mighty. The following day we explored Central Park, Rockefeller Center, sauntered down Fifth Avenue, and had lunch in the SoHo District with Julia Ratcliffe. Julia and my daughter, Heather, had been Rotary Exchange students in 1988—Heather first visiting Julia at her home in Hertford, England, and, later, Julia with all of us in California—and I had come to think of her as another daughter. Julia was now a structural engineer, temporarily based in New York, and it was wonderful to meet up again and introduce her to Noel. We had a delicious lunch with lots of lively chat and laughter. We took a very long walk back to our hotel from SoHo, absorbing the feel of the city.

That evening, as our taxi approached the Metropolitan Opera House at Lincoln Center, our breaths caught in anticipation. We walked through the foyer of the Met feeling like school kids in a candy shop. Mammoth chandeliers hung over the mosaic of colorfully dressed music lovers. In the concert hall my first impression was staggering. The gigantic gold curtain stretched across the stage and seemed to flow into the ceiling and the room was illuminated with crystal prisms, causing rainbows to dance on the ceiling. We found our seats, sat down, and soaked in the warmth of the moment. Each red plush seat had a small screen on the back so one could read the subtitles of the opera in English. The orchestra was warming up and the room was abuzz with energy.

A woman sitting in front of me suddenly turned. "Excuse me," she said. "Your dress is lovely. Who is the designer?"

"Oh, I don't know, I'm sorry. But thank you," I said, stifling a giggle. I had bought the dress at Robinson's May on sale for thirty dollars. Noel and I would often laugh over that in the years to come.

The lights dimmed and a hush fell over the audience as the overture began. Noel caressed my hand as the curtain opened, and we began to absorb the sights, sounds, and colors of 1840s Parisian life. The multitude of costumed actors, from street urchins to fashionable aristocrats—oh, and the live elephants, and horses on stage, were fantastic. From the tenors to the soprano the voices were heavenly as Giacomo Puccini's tragic love story unfolded, and tears silently slid down my cheeks. Noel was right—*La Boheme* was the perfect choice for my first step, or, perhaps, leap, into the world of opera.

After the performance, too wound up to sleep, we returned to Rosie O'Grady's. Just like your local pub in Ireland, we were greeted as regulars. As we sat, Puccini's music still swirling in our heads, we spoke of the opera and the evening's magical moments. During his twenties, Noel had studied voice for opera and musical theater. He owned a large collection of opera recordings. Now we had fulfilled his dream of seeing an opera at The Met, together.

The next morning we returned to North Carolina, where we spent Easter weekend with Yvette and Gary. Jeff and Andrea joined us, as did the Kilgores' twin boys and daughter. On Easter morning, Yvette and I suddenly decided to do an old-fashioned egg hunt for our grown children. The kids thought we were crazy and acted as though they cared less about the hunt, but we went ahead and bought plastic eggs and filled them with candy and coins. Yvette, Noel and I went out to hide the eggs in the garden. Then I noticed that Noel was on his knees, digging a shallow hole and preparing to drop in one of the eggs. I asked what he was doing.

"Hiding the eggs!" he replied cheerfully.

"In the dirt? They'll never find them!" I said, laughing.

"But aren't they supposed to hunt for them? Isn't this what you're supposed to do? I've never done an Easter egg hunt."

I figured that everyone knew how to hide Easter eggs, but apparently not. So Yvette and I explained the hunt: You did not dig in the ground to hide the eggs. You hid them behind plants, in trees, between the hose, and under patio cushions. After the eggs were properly hidden, we called our kids, who were watching television inside the house. They came reluctantly, scoffing at the childish game. But as soon as we said, "Go!" their competitive spirits took over and they became like little kids searching for the golden egg. We all had a great laugh out of Noel's hiding the eggs in the dirt. But it was the beginning of many Easter egg hunts.

Noel had to fly back to Ireland, and I had to return to California. We again said our sad farewells at the airport. We wanted to be together all the time and often spoke about how we could accomplish this as quickly as possible. I was just thankful that the phone company had special rates to Ireland, as we were able to speak for hours, without thoughts of going bankrupt. We had lots of plans for the rest of the year. Noel would return in June for a couple of weeks. He would miss Wendy and Andy's wedding at the end of July. Although invited, he had business commitments in Ireland. In September we would tour Ireland with the Kilgores and the Bovards. And though we had yet to plan for it, I was sure we would be together again for Christmas.

When Noel returned in June, I had good news to share. I had stayed in touch with Chrystal, my former student at Orangewood. I sometimes struggled to explain the effect Chrystal had on my life. I had always known that if Teri was unable to get custody of Chrystal that I would try. At her sixth grade graduation, it was clear that Chrystal had affected so many others, too. I always told her she was going to make a huge difference in this world. Now I could report that Chrystal had escaped the legal system. Teri had been able to adopt her. We had kept in touch, and I could not wait for Noel to meet her. We drove to Redlands, where they lived now as a family, and took Chrystal to lunch. Noel and Chrystal hit it off right away, as I suspected they would. He loved her spunk and her ability to survive. Over the years, they would joke back and forth, always finding something to laugh about. Noel joined me as part of Chrystal's fan club.

We Have to Break Up

January 11. 2001. "No, you don't have to come, Noel," I said, as I parked the car at the Irvine Hoag Medical Center. "It's just a routine mammogram and won't take long. You can't come into the room with me anyway, so you may as well stay here in the sunshine and read."

"Routine mammogram." As I lay on the exam table, my words echoed in my head. There was nothing routine about it. The ultra-sound technician had left the screen lit, showing the foreboding black spot within my left breast, while he located the radiologist. Early in December, I had discovered a small lump in my breast. Playing down my gut suspicion, I ignored it through the holidays, not wanting to worry family and friends needlessly during this joyous time, though I told Noel about it.

Now the reality of the tiny black spot overwhelmed me, and I feared it would change my days and new life. The radiologist came in and clicked off the screen. His demeanor was solemn as he told me that I should call my gynecologist as soon as possible.

"I am so sorry to tell you this", he said with compassion in his voice. "Wish I had better news."

"Oh," I swallowed deeply, "It's OK. I feel bad for you having to tell me that news. I'm sure I'll be fine. Thank you."

I hurriedly dressed, a feeling of gloom enveloping me.

Pull yourself together, I thought, *before you see Noel.* I walked out into the sunlight, thinking that everything looked the same, though my world had just shifted again. Just another thing in my life. Another lesson to learn, another mountain to climb. Now I'll have to tell people. I don't want my kids to worry. Guess I just want a perfect life. But Wendy, too, had recently found a lump in her breast that the doctor said they would watch. Maybe I could get her checked here. And I really did not want Noel to have to navigate the medical world again, as he had with Mary.

"Sorry it took so long," I said to Noel as I opened the car door.

"That's all right. I've been reading and enjoying the sun." (Sun in January was a rare treat for an Irishman). "How are you?" he said, looking at me closely.

"They verified the lump. They found it on the mammogram and then gave me an ultrasound. The radiologist wants me to call my gynecologist, Dr. Lawrence Klein, immediately and see a surgeon. He thinks it's breast cancer," I said tearfully.

"Oh, Annie. I'm so sorry. I should have been with you. You shouldn't have been alone." Noel grasped my hand.

"Oh, I'm OK," I said and shakily reached for the key in the ignition. Then I stopped and said the words I had been rehearsing whenever I thought the lump might be cancer. "We have to break up, Noel. You need to go back home to Ireland."

Noel was stunned. "Why? We love each other."

"Because you went through all those years of illness with Mary. It's just not fair for you to have another sick woman on your hands. I won't do that to you."

"Annie, look at me," Noel demanded.

I turned and looked into his eyes.

Noel quietly said, "I am here in all times, not just the good. That's what love is. We love each other. We will deal with it together. And please don't ever say that to me again. I would never leave you. You are stuck with me!"

More tears sprang to my eyes as we silently hugged. I was not sure what my future was, but at least Noel would be in it with me.

* * * * *

After Dr. Klein read my ultrasound, he referred me to Dr. Alice Police, a surgeon specializing in breast cancer at Hoag Hospital, for a biopsy. The following week Noel, Heather, and I sat in Dr. Police's office. Heather had come to the appointment armed with books, information, and questions. Her documentary on breast cancer, *Choosing Hope*, had screened in 1999. The film follows three women on their journey with breast cancer at three different facilities, UCLA, the City of Hope, and Hoag. I felt so bad for her as she knew so much about breast cancer, and one of the women in the documentary had died; now she was dealing with her mother's diagnosis. I was sure Heather was terrified, but she went stoically forward with her questions. She was instrumental in my choosing Hoag as the best place to fight my cancer. Heather was with me as Dr. Police explained the procedure for a biopsy.

"We just take a little of the tissue, send it to pathology, and determine if it is benign or cancerous," she explained.

"It's a simple procedure. We can do it right here, or schedule for another time."

I looked at Heather. "I guess you can do it now." I said quietly.

We left the office, me with a small bandage over my incision and the dread of waiting for the results. I was thankful for Heather's knowledge and take-charge manner and Noel's strength and quiet reassurance. As the enormity of what I might be facing began to sink in, I decided to keep a journal of my journey through cancer.

January 22. Waited all day Monday until Dr. Police called to say, "You have a little cancer."

"A little cancer?" Either you do or do not!

But the doctor's voice was reassuring as she gave me an encouraging report. The cancer was small and had been detected early, so it was probably not in my lymph nodes. It was treatable, though I did not need a mastectomy. "More doesn't mean better," she explained. She wanted to perform a lumpectomy and a sentinel node biopsy, as quickly as possible.

I was shaky when I got off the phone. I had heard all the positive things Dr. Police had said but really only focused on the word *"cancer."* I reported what Dr. Police said to Noel, who was supportive and positive. He wanted to go to the next appointment, and when I called Heather, she did, too. Then I called Wendy in Rohnert Park, Jeff in Nashville, and Mom. I could hear the upset in Mom's voice. But the best way I could help her with her feelings was by being positive. Later Jim called, very upset. He never could handle illness well, and he sounded so sad. He didn't want me to go through this—was there anything I needed? Strange how things work out. Jim always took so much energy from me. With Noel I didn't feel the need to protect him or hide bad news from him. I just accepted his calm reassurance. Lucky me.

January 31. The day of surgery loomed. First, a radioactive substance, or blue dye, would be injected into the tumor. The dye would then travel to the lymph nodes, alerting the surgeon as to which one was the first (sentinel) node in the chain. This eliminated the need to unnecessarily remove all the lymph nodes. The procedure would take between thirty minutes and four hours. Mom, Betty, and Noel said they would be waiting when I got out of surgery.

In my case the dye traveled quickly to the nodes. Within thirty minutes I had dressed and went to find Mom, Betty, and Noel. Nobody was in the waiting room. I searched the entire hospital, from the cafeteria to other waiting rooms, until I just sat down and read my book. About an hour later they came walking down the hall. Expecting the procedure to take an hour or more, they had gone to Denny's for breakfast. It made me laugh as they promised to be there, no matter what.

At one o'clock I underwent the sentinel lymph node lumpectomy, in which Dr. Police removed the tumor and two lymph nodes, which were immediately checked for cancer. Afterward I could hear people talking but was still drowsy. Finally a voice said, "Wake up. Your surgery is over."

I opened my eyes and saw Noel and Heather.

Then I heard the reassuring words: "They did not find it in your lymph nodes. They took out the tumor. You will be fine."

Over the next few days I rested, grateful for only a small amount of discomfort. I knew I faced radiation but felt hopeful, since they had not found cancer in my lymph nodes, that I would not need chemotherapy. Noel continually fussed over me—funny how he knew instinctively what I needed. I felt thankful and lucky.

We gardened, watched movies—*Guys and Dolls* was on TV one evening, and cooked, and I decided that God really does work in mysterious ways. I was thankful for His guidance, direction, and unplanned surprises. Knowledge unlocks the void of blackness, and I was lucky to have Heather's knowledge and understanding. She had been my ears through this journey, as I came to see that one doesn't hear everything correctly when it is your own body and new terms can be hard to grasp. I also found it amazing that I, always the one to arm myself with information, feared even looking on the Internet—as if I could pretend ignorance of my cancer. It was still hard to realize that I suffered from a life threatening condition.

February 3. Wendy and Heather came for dinner, along with Mom. The menu was ham, stuffed potatoes, salad, and strawberries. With the girls' assistance, Noel took charge of the kitchen, where they talked and giggled as they worked. They asked Noel when he would return. (His three-month visa would end on February 12.) It seemed to me that they liked him more these days, that they were becoming friends. After dinner we played cards. Noel was extremely attentive, watchful of when I tired or needed water. What a lovely feeling, as I had never had this before.

The following days were filled with doctor's visits interspersed with rest and visits with Noel to local sights—the town circle in Orange, milkshakes at Watson's coffee shop (opened in 1899), Mass at the San Fernando Mission—and oh, yes, the apologetic news from Dr. Police that cancer had, in fact, been detected in the lymph nodes. As we planned the attack (chemotherapy and radiation), I kept reminding myself that I could take a positive or a negative approach to my treatments. Having cancer was not my choice but how I dealt with it was. We met with Dr. Vandermolen, an oncologist who had appeared in Heather's documentary, *Choosing Hope,* to set up the necessary tests before my first chemotherapy on February 14. We also stopped by St. Matthew's Church in Orange, a Catholic church that we had been told permits a Catholic to marry a divorcee. However this turned out to be an ecumenical Catholic church that did not answer to the Pope, which did not fit in with Noel's belief system.

And then Noel's three months were up again. I hated packing for his return, and even Bentley, who was loosing his primary ball thrower, turned glum. At LAX we reminisced over Christmas and the best New Year's Eve Noel said he ever had, and laughed, always the laughter. Then his plane was aloft and I drove home, where Bentley greeted me and went looking for Noel.

I thought of all the changes 2001 had brought. My breast had gone from a sexual to a medical object of interest. It was amazing, all the cards, letters, care and concern I had received, yet reflected in everyone's eyes was *cancer!* which I hated. Having cancer makes everyone react differently to you. Noel understood this so well. Distressed that he could not be with me through the treatments, he emailed, "Annie, I am not gone, I am still with you, now and forever love!!!" He called often, sometimes waking me in the morning. He said the two saddest times in his life were when Mary died and when he left me that Friday at the airport. Wow, how could anyone love me that much? God had given me a priceless gift when he brought Noel into my life. He allowed me to see unconditional love in the flesh.

Valentine's Day was my first day of chemotherapy. I checked my calendar and saw that Noel had written, "I love you," which brought tears to my eyes. In my journal I wrote, "Today is the day—the beginning of a journey through medical craziness, though with wonderful, caring professionals." Unsure of what to expect I put on my best game face. The nurses turned out to be fabulous. They gave me lots of meds to combat the nausea that comes with chemotherapy. When they put up the Adryomycin drip, which was red, I remembered Noel's good-humored approach to life, and joked, " Is that chemo red because it's Valentine's Day? Will it be green for St. Patrick's Day?"

But the chemo wracked my body and mind; hot flashes swept over me. *How ironic*, I thought, as my menopausal self had once declared, "Oh, yes, definitely I want hormone replacement therapy. I would rather have breast cancer than hot flashes." Now I had both, as well as sleeplessness, aches deep into the bone, coughing, nausea, and plain weariness. Not to mention hair loss, which I expected, but it was still odd to have my hair peel off my scalp. My head felt so cold; my scalp felt like a skinned knee. Luckily Noel had insisted that we look for wigs before he left for Ireland. We had great fun at the wig shop, laughing at my options: Should I try a new look? Long blonde hair? Go redhead? I finally chose wigs that looked pretty much like my normal hair, along with hats and scarves. These scarves were a gift from a woman in Heather's documentary, who gave me a lesson in scarf tying, though I never did master that skill. Mom wanted to bring me to her house, which I declined. I wanted my independence. One evening I watched the movie *Who Was Joe Gould?,* coming away with the insight that real history is what we say and do, a reflection of who we are. It was time to read, meditate, and heal. I visualized the cancer cells floating through my bloodstream being gobbled up by the little Pac Men of chemotherapy, and, in the future, scorched by radiation treatments. Friends and family checked in to encourage and, always, Noel's quiet spirit was with me: his humor, his good sense, his balance, and his laughter. Cancer showed me what exceptional friends I had: a circle of friendship filled with prayer, laughter, strength, positive energy, tears, joy, pain, and, at its core, love.

Ruby Avenue

arch 3. Leased a house on Balboa Island! As Mom said, "It's a place to heal." It was also closer to Hoag. I was happy to be moving back from Mission Hills in the San Fernando Valley. At the time I thought it was a good idea to move to a town home in a less expensive area, where I could substitute teach, but I missed the beach terribly.

Listen to your body and your spirit, I now told myself. *For once honor your body and give it the best chance to fight this cancer invasion. Think of yourself—only.* Oh, but I found that last idea difficult. In the midst of everything, Noel called from Ireland with great news. He received an offer to buy his barbershop in Douglas. He also planned to return to California on April thirteenth. One good thing about my cancer diagnosis: I could actually feel how much I was loved and cared for.

March 13. Moved to the Island! Amazing how settled I already feel. I know I will be happier here by the beach. I talked to Noel before I went to sleep. Only thirty-one days before he returns.

In the weeks that followed, Mom came down to help me unpack. She still fussed over me—her worry was palpable—but I determined to live a normal, independent life through my treatments. One day I came across two photographs of my grandmothers, beautiful women in their twenties. I hung their pictures to remind me of their legacies. Gramma Mary gave me the love of reading. Nana gave me my love of travel. She always said she was Irish, and though I have been unable to make the genealogical connection, to me she will always be Irish.

Between chores I walked the Island with Bentley, who loved being back in his old territory, and, oh yes, *really* tried to make time to rest. *Take it easy, Annie,* I told myself. *Remember you have limits now. Cancer allows you to rest and to let others help you.* One afternoon while I was out with Bentley, Noel called, and Mom took the message off the machine. "Annie," she said, when I returned. "Noel called and said he loves you."

It was difficult for her to say it, and I probably blushed when I heard her relay the message, but perhaps she was beginning to understand the depth of our relationship. Meanwhile, the aches and sleeplessness continued, and the never-ending appointments with oncologists, MRIs, and blood work. It was hard to imagine adding radiation to my calendar. Sometimes, when I thought about what chemo was already doing to my body, it scared me badly. I tried to compartmentalize those feelings, a great form of denial.

April 2. These days I sometimes found myself fighting everything in my life, or, should I say, fighting the cancer. Maybe it sounds silly but I felt more in control of my life if I kept to my normal routine, even to the point of exhaustion.

Noel closed his business on April seventh. I felt terribly guilty that he had changed his entire life for me. No one had ever given up so much for me. People kept asking whether we were going to marry, but I did not really know what was going to happen. Amazing how love changes after age fifty. Noel was a decent, caring, compassionate, and funny man. I loved him. All the obstacles really did not matter, as each day was wonderfully happier with him in my life. When I talked to Noel he sounded happy and said he looked forward to seeing me. I remember how upset he got when I told him he had to go back to Ireland and find someone else. His response: "That is what love is, not just the good times," still echoed in my mind.

And then Noel's sale fell through—the buyer did not want the shop until the end of June. One more obstacle. I felt sad for him, as he had been so happy to be retiring, and wondered, *What journey are we on now?*

When Noel arrived on the thirteenth, he didn't seem to mind my hairless look, and he liked the wig and hat I was wearing. Then he hugged me. On the drive home from LAX he said that the Irish government had verified that his insurance fund and pension could be direct-deposited to his Irish bank account, even if he permanently moved to the United States. (At his first inquiry, he had been told he would not be eligible to receive that money if he moved to another country.)

Mom and her friend, Betty Dooley, came for dinner that night. Noel egged them on about many issues, especially politics. He admired our president, Bill Clinton, which did not sit well with my staunch Republican mother. He also criticized our health-care system. Mom took great offense to the conversation, as she was not used to the European way of discussing another's ideas and opinions without taking it personally. One thing I've observed about Ireland is that the pub serves as a great place to chat, share opinions and beliefs, discuss the day's events, and still leave as friends. People can, and often do, have varying opinions—that is the joy of the conversation.

With Noel back I felt centered and grounded again. We did mundane things together—shopping, walking, and cooking, but each moment seemed meaningful because he was there to share it. One day we wandered Fashion Island to window-shop. I remembered our first visit to that shopping center, when Noel commented on all the grandfathers and their "daughters" pushing baby strollers. I had laughed. "That's not their daughters—that's their new wives."

He was flabbergasted. At the Green Thumb nursery in Lake Forest we bought Mom new patio chair covers and plants for Mother's Day. That Friday Noel installed the plants and her new covers. The day after Mother's Day, Mom confided in Noel that she thought he was good for me. Wow, what a huge understatement, though truly remarkable coming from Mom, who had not trusted Noel at all when they first met. She also informed us that she and Betty had postponed their visit to Boise to see Betty's family. With Noel having to return to Ireland, she thought I would need her.

June. Fourteenth day of radiation, only sixteen more to go. It's funny that they tell you to have thirty consecutive visits, except weekend and holidays, and you must come at the same time each day. The radiologist "tattooed" me with tiny round dots in the area to be radiated, then a lead shield was placed surrounding the area of my breast where the lump had been removed. The first week of radiation had been difficult; looking in the mirror was scary. No hair, a black X on my breast, lying exposed on the table in the oversized white room that housed the radiation equipment. I again had to get my mindset in OK mode: *This is just a phase; it does not matter.* Luckily Noel had been with me for the first few treatments and kept saying it made no difference whether or not I had hair, I was me. Then he had to return to Ireland, and I returned to radiation alone.

When Noel arrived in July, we celebrated the Fourth, his first, with a barbecue for sixteen (Noel was getting good at barbecuing), a parade, and fireworks. The Fourth is my favorite holiday—I have hosted an annual parade at my house, wherever we were, since 1979—as it is a relaxed time for family and friends, good fun, no presents, no pressure, old-fashioned ice cream sundaes, and fireworks. This year, however, I tweaked my left knee, tearing the meniscus. This injury was much more painful and intrusive than the breast cancer. I faced arthroscopic surgery and pleaded with the radiologist, oncologist, and orthopedic surgeon to operate right away, but it could not and would not be done until the radiation treatments were finished. August seemed a long time away. Even though my knee hurt, Noel and I continued to have fun. We went to the Hollywood Bowl, had a picnic and enjoyed the music under the stars, drove along the coast—always stopping to take in the breathtaking beauty of the sea, and just enjoyed the simplest moments with each other. We even drove to the family condominium in Gull Lake, where we met Betty and Mom on their return trip from Idaho. It was gorgeous up there and, although the stairs were steep to navigate, I enjoyed the majesty of the mountains and the calmness of the lakes and streams.

After Noel left for Ireland, I slumped into sadness. So much going on, and I needed to sort out my life. Although the chemotherapy and radiation were finished, I saw Dr. Vandermolen monthly, underwent blood tests to check my cancer markers and other tests to check for any changes in my body, and ingested Tamoxifin daily to insure that the cancer did not return. I found it ironic that I had believed Dr. Police in January when she said she got all the cancer, and then listened to the oncologist say, "Yes, she got it all. But you need chemo and radiation. And then a five year treatment of Tamoxifin."

I needed to believe I truly was cured to be able to go forward with my life. I fretted over what the future held, with random thoughts and scenarios careening through my head until I was plain exhausted. To make sense of it all, I made a timeline of all that had happened over the last four years: a separation and divorce after a thirty-year marriage, selling our family home of twenty years, the changing dynamics of our family life, moving to Balboa Island, traveling to Ireland and meeting Noel, returning to teaching, Jeff and Andrea's wedding in Alabama, falling in love with Noel, Dad's death, Wendy's wedding, moving to the Valley, breast cancer, moving back to Balboa Island, surgery, chemotherapy, radiation, and now knee surgery. And always, Noel's visits— seven trips in 2001 alone. No wonder I was overwhelmed. *Stop, Annie!* I told myself. *Enjoy the moments.*

9/11: A Symbol of My Life

September 11, 2001. The ringing phone shattered my dream. I looked at the clock: 6:22 a.m. and wondered who was calling this early as I stumbled down the hall to get the phone.

"Isn't it terrible?" Mom said, her ordinarily firm voice shaky.

"Isn't what terrible?"

"Aren't you watching the news?" she said. "An airplane just hit a skyscraper in New York City. They think it's a terrorist attack."

I turned on the television. Manhattan's tallest buildings, the twin towers of the World Trade Center, set against the backdrop of a crystal blue sky, were billowing smoke. I stumbled through the conversation as Mom and I tried to make sense of what was happening. She recalled her shock when Pearl Harbor was bombed in 1941, throwing the United States into war. She never thought it could happen again. Now our country was under attack, and we didn't know why.

As Noel emerged from the hallway, I pointed at the television screen. As he always did, Noel turned to me to see how I was doing, then sat down on the couch, stunned. Wanting to be alone with him, I said, "Mom, I'll call you later. Love you."

Noel and I stared at the changing sounds and images on the screen—ordinary people and extraordinary heroes, running to and from the smoke, the crumbling towers, and the wailing sirens of fire engines and police cars as news anchors and cameramen scrambled to make sense of it all.

The phone rang again. Noel's brother, Mick, in Ireland. "Are you two all right?"

"Yes," I said quickly. "Here's Noel," and passed the phone. I was not up for talking right then. As my eyes remained glued to the ever-changing images on the screen, I half listened until Noel said good-bye.

"Mick was worried," Noel said in his calm voice as he grasped my hand. "Irish television is also covering this. He can't believe it."

I phoned each of my children, wanting to connect with the family and make sure that each one was all right. I spoke with each of them, struggling to sort out what we were watching. The phone continued to ring throughout the day, a lifeline to the ones we loved. Family and friends, locally and from across the U.S. and Ireland called to talk. Each conversation gave us a bit of normalcy and the assurance of what was important in life. We all felt the world was about to change because of this event, though we could not yet know how and to what extent.

At first Americans pulled together as one. Our country had been attacked, and a united spirit cloaked our land. Then came the urge to retaliate, the drive for retribution, as we embarked upon the search for Osama Bin Laden and his Al Qaeda co-conspirators. The cost of our wars in Iraq and Afghanistan would cause our national debt to skyrocket.

The Department of Homeland Security was organized. The lines grew long at airport security checkpoints. Many people grew suspicious of their fellow Muslim Americans; immigrants were looked upon as a threat to our nation's safety.

On September 11 our country lost its complacency. Many became aware that moments count. Each life lost that day was commemorated by family and friends, who expressed regret that they had spent more time with their loved one, said "I love you" more often, laughed more, traveled more, and cherished the moments of each day.

As I reflected on that day when so much changed, I realized that my personal 9/11 begun a few years earlier. My hopes, dreams, and expectations had crumbled, blindsided by something outside my control. During that string of catastrophes, I learned how to live. We may plan for the future, but plans can change in an instant, so we must always live in the moment. Some of those moments can turn magical. My own change of plans had sent me on a journey to an obscure pub on the Connemara coast of Ireland, where I met the love of my life. As someone said, "Once in a while, right in the middle of an ordinary life, love gives us a fairy tale."

My 9/11 epiphany came when I accepted the magic of each moment. I made a positive choice to live in the moment, for each one is precious and we never get it back. The survivors of September eleventh understand that so well. Noel and I, too, were living that philosophy, cramming adventure into each day. We had traveled, laughed, talked, and explored the world of ideas, so we never feared having regrets. Now, whenever I signed off on an email, I add, "Enjoy the Moments."

A Funeral, Two Weddings, Three Houses, and a Baby

*T*he year 2002 dawned with anticipation. For one, there was Heather's June wedding in Louisville, Kentucky. But as Time Square's New Year's ball dropped into 2002, I had no idea of how many more life-changing events would occur over these next twelve months.

February. Noel and I began shopping for a house. We knew we were always going to be together and wanted a permanent home, not a rental. Although we loved Balboa Island, it was too pricey for our pocketbook. We both wanted to be near the coast, so we looked in Newport Beach, Costa Mesa, Turtle Rock in Irvine, and Huntington Beach. None of these places felt comfortable. Almost daily we would approach the intersection of Bayside Drive and Pacific Coast Highway (PCH), always turning left onto PCH. We often saw a For Sale sign peeking over the brick wall on the other side of the highway. One day we decided to continue across PCH to see just what was for sale in this area. DeAnza Bayside Village is a mobile home park, with a marina, two swimming pools, two clubhouses, and a workout room. We drove the streets, taking down several phone numbers of places for sale. We inquired at the office, where we learned that the mobile and modular homes sat on leased land. But the neighborhood seemed perfect for us—affordable mobile homes, an affordable monthly lease, and the perfect lifestyle location near the Back Bay and the Island. We were shown a mobile home at a fabulous price, with an extended lease until 2026. The owner, a retired Irvine policeman, had lived in the unit less than six months. He hated the mobile home, did not want to fix it up, and wanted to sell the property "as is." Well, one man's trash is another's treasure. We made an offer and were thrilled when it was accepted. We planned to move in on the first of April, but wanted to paint and carpet first. Heather and Derek and Wendy and Andy all helped out. Mom and Betty even came by to supervise. No one in the family seemed quite sure about our move to a mobile home, and I kidded that I now was real trailer trash—a comment that was not accepted as funny. But Noel and I never cared about prestige or appearances; we just went with what felt right to us. We were happy to be putting down roots. We moved in on April first, hoping we would not prove to be fools.

March. A simple phone call from Jeff and Andrea changed our life again. Jeff and Andrea had just returned from a family trip to Sicily, and when they called I heard the excitement in Jeff's voice. "Mom, we're going to have a baby!" he blurted out. "Andrea is due the end of November or beginning of December. She just went to the doctor today."

My first grandchild! My heart seemed to expand. "Oh, Jeff, I'm thrilled. How exciting. I'm so happy for you and Andrea. How is she feeling?"

"She's great, Mom. We're so excited we can't believe It.," he stammered.

As I hung up, I thought, *Now we have three events to celebrate: a wedding, a new home and a new baby.*

April. Mom's cough had lingered since Christmas. In the midst of many X-rays, medications, and treatments, she had managed to finish a queen-sized wedding quilt for Heather and Derek and was working on a baby quilt for Jeff and Andrea. Meanwhile she continued to play eighteen holes of golf, and run the family business. She was packed and ready to leave on a Panama Canal cruise on the sixth, until her internist called with the results of her recent MRI. Mom had Stage IV lung cancer. When she heard the diagnosis. Mom almost collapsed, and my sister, Lynda, and I brought her home, all of us in shock. So began our quick and intense horror of a journey through terminal cancer. The next day we met with the oncologist who had seen Lynda through breast cancer. There was no treatment for Stage IV lung cancer, aside from an experimental program. It either worked in the first week or it did not work at all.

"Would you like to try the experimental program?" the doctor asked.

"I guess so. If that is the only option," Mom said shakily. She had always been the one in charge. Now her choices were being stripped away.

We discovered quickly that the program did not work and had to face the reality that Mom was dying. She had been hospitalized only twice that I could remember, for a thyroid problem in the early 1950s and a hysterectomy in the 1960s. Mom was always positive and energetic, the matriarch and foundation of our family. Dad sometimes called her "Sarge," as she was always in charge. She had taken over the family business when her own father developed dementia in the late 1960s and had earned the respect and admiration of her peers as the business prospered. My children had never seen their grandmother in bed or sick. Now the transition was astoundingly rapid. She still managed all of her accounts, spoke with her financial advisor and her lawyer, and visited with friends and family. She turned to Steve Metcalf to help organize her funeral, and gave me direction as to how the family business should be run. (In 1991 I had begun to work with her so as to have someone in the family ready should Mom decide to step down, though I never, ever imagined that happening.)

We called in hospice. Noel and I stayed at her house, as did Heather. Wendy had just started a new job but visited often. Jeff and Andrea arrived from Nashville. We were able to remind Mom of our love and reminisce. It was a bittersweet time, given Heather's upcoming wedding and the need to go over the plans, all the while knowing that Mom would not be with us. Jeff and Andrea's baby would be Mom's sixth great-grandchild, and she would not be with us to share that joyous event either. I must say something about Noel during this difficult time. He brought all of us comfort with his quiet demeanor, his soft Irish voice, and his presence. He spent hours by Mom's bedside. Once I awoke in the middle of the night and saw him just sitting there, holding her hand. He just wanted her to know someone was awake and that we were there. Only later did I learn that during one of these moments Mom had asked Noel to take care of me. I found this amazing, as she had been suspicious, unkind, and pettily obnoxious to him when they first met. She had worried that he was after my money, while Noel's family thought I was a gold-digger from America. Yet money was never a topic of discussion when we were together.

May. One month and five days from her diagnosis, Mom passed away peacefully, surrounded by her family. She lived her final moments as she had lived her life, with dignity and grace. At the time we were all stunned by the quick finality of that month, though I later realized that she had a perfect death. She endured little pain—just extreme shortness of breath at the end, which was manageable with morphine, no needless surgeries, and no hospitalization. We all had time to say a loving good bye to our mom, grandma, sister, aunt, and friend. Mom had left me a final gift when she asked Noel to take care of me, as I knew I finally had her blessing to marry.

Later in May, Noel and I drove cross-country to Louisville for Heather and Derek's wedding. We packed the favors, gifts, miscellaneous wedding paraphernalia, suitcases, and, most important, the wedding dress into our Ford Escape. We were off on another adventure, a timely break from the intense moments of the past few weeks, which had been filled with business, banking, sorting paperwork, and learning all that was crucial to taking over the running of the business. Her shoes were too big to fill, though, and I often doubted my ability to do all that was needed. Noel was always there to encourage, support, discuss, and hold my hand, my calm reassurance in the face of constant change.

We drove eastward, listening to music, audio books, talking, laughing, and sightseeing. In Ireland everyone talks about the Grand Canyon, and Noel was thrilled to see it for himself. He loved the depth and beauty of the canyon, snapping numerous pictures as the light danced and weaved on the cliffs. At the canyon's edge, I got the wedding dress out and took a picture to show Heather that we were in constant contact with the dress. (In the parking lot someone asked whether I was going to throw the dress over the cliff, as many jilted brides have done. Noel and I chuckled.) At a garage sale in Albuquerque we bought a silly little brass bell, etched with flowers and leaves, which turned out to be useful years later. In Joplin, Missouri, we found the house where my maternal grandfather was born. This was an historical house with a large plaque adorning the front stating that it had been built in the early 1890s. I looked at the "Z," which stood for Zelliken, still etched into the glass entry door. Noel encouraged me to knock at the door and ask if we could view the house. We were invited in and I got to see the downstairs of this massive mansion.

Noel loved seeing mid-America, with its small towns, expanses of prairie, and never-ending highways. At night we would search out a hotel and a restaurant, where we often spoke with locals about their area. In St. Louis we stayed with my friend, Debbie Mason. Unfortunately her husband, Bill, was out of town but we had a wonderful evening of dinner, wine, and conversation. Debbie, too, fell under Noel's charm and quiet ways, and the two became instant friends. Each night Noel and I carried the wedding dress into our room along with our suitcases. Along the way we often sang or made up games. One favorite was "Name That Tune;" however, after one long day's drive, I was silly and asked Noel to name the tune in one note.

"One note?" he said laughing.

"Yes, one note! Ready?" I asked, and hummed the note.

He looked at me like I was crazy but guessed a song.

"Nope," I laughed. "Try again," and repeated the note, after which I laughed even harder.

He guessed again. Wrong!

But on the third try, he said "Happy Birthday."

"Right!" I said, before dissolving into laughter. We played that game and throughout that trip and on many of our drives over the years, always falling into laughter at the craziness of trying to guess the right song in one note.

June. We arrived in Louisville on the fifth, rested and refreshed. As we checked into the Drury Inn & Suites, Heather and Derek appeared with others in the other wedding party. The celebration was beginning early, and it seemed, at least for this week, that the sadness and turmoil of the last couple of months had been left behind in California. Friends and family continued to arrive, last minute errands were run, the tuxedos picked up, bridesmaids dresses pressed and waiting, the wedding gown safely hung, and the wedding rehearsal dinner accomplished.

Heather's wedding day dawned. Her wedding was simple and elegant, small and intimate. It was held in the garden of Running Water Farm, with the only unplanned glitch being the hot and humid weather. Bride and groom radiated happiness. (They each wore an angel representing their grandmothers, as Derek's grandmother was too ill to attend.) The reception by the pool and the buffet, with the Hot Brown, the open-faced turkey-and-bacon sandwich topped with Mornay sauce made famous by the city's historic Brown Hotel, was scrumptious. Yvette and Gary and Joan and Ken attended the wedding, and we all had such fun together. Suddenly the day was over, and Heather and Derek were ready to leave. They were staying at the Brown Hotel, but would return in the morning for a farewell brunch Noel and I were to host. The limo arrived and Heather and Derek ran to the car with a confetti of white rose petals floating through the air, cheers of well-wishers resonating in their ears, and love and happiness filling the air. As Noel and I held hands, he wiped away my joyous tears as the happy pair drove off.

As June ninth dawned, Noel and I were up early to set up the buffet, planned for ten o'clock. Given everyone's various flight times, destinations, and plans for Sunday, we thought they could have a bit of breakfast and leave at their leisure in the afternoon. Then Wendy told us that Andy changed his flight and would leave in fifteen minutes. Noel and I looked at each other. We made a quick decision. We asked the kids to follow us into the hall for a moment. As the kids surrounded us, Noel put his hands up.

"I have something to say to all of you. We were going

to wait until later, but since Andy is leaving in a minute and we want tell you all together, we decided to do it right now," Noel said, with a twinkle in his eye as he grabbed my left hand.

He reached into his pocket and took out a small box. "I have asked your mom to marry me. We want to make it official and for you to be the first to know," he said as he removed the ring and placed it on the fourth finger of my left hand. "Also, you are not really the first to know," he added. "I spoke with your grandmother before she died, and she gave me her blessing."

Mom had blessed our engagement? I was stunned. And then the kids erupted with whoops of joy along with much hugging, congratulations, and tears. We made so much noise that some of our friends came into the hall. Our joy followed us back in to the brunch, where we were congratulated and hugged again. We were officially engaged. All we had to do was set a date.

July. A Home in Ballycotton. When Noel returned to Ireland, I joined him to help pack up, as his house in Douglas had finally sold. I had encouraged him to find another house in Ireland, which we could call home. He toyed with the idea of adding a small unit on his property, looked at a unit in Shannon near his brother, and scoured the papers for good deals. Noel's dream had always been to live near the coast. Between packing boxes, we took long drives, where Noel showed me the special places he knew. One day we drove to Youghal to look at an apartment on the water. When we arrived, we did not even go in to inquire. It was disappointingly unkempt. Then we spotted a For Sale sign on a unit next to a funeral parlor, which, we joked, would be a perfect neighbor. We parked and decided to take a short walk. As we rounded the corner I noticed a real estate flyer in a window. It showed a housing complex with views of the ocean and included a floor plan.

"Wow, where is this?" I said.

"Oh, that's near Sean's pub in Ballycotton. But Sean said it is not built well and not worth the money." Sean, Mary's brother, is a McGrath, and I had met him and his wife, Denise, on an earlier visit.

"But look at the view. Let's go see it," I said excitedly.

It was a twenty-minute drive to Ballycotton, a village that can cast spell. In 1995, Hollywood producers chose the village as the location for a film called *Divine Rapture*. The script was full of blarney—a cataleptic woman suddenly returns to life, restoring the fortunes of the local priest. Then another miracle occurs—mackerel fall from the sky! The cast was stellar—Marlon Brando, as the red-haired priest, John Hurt, Deborah Winger, and Johnny Depp. When he arrived in Ireland, Brando said that he felt an immediate connection, as though he had come home. The film would likely have made Ballycotton famous, but the financing turned out to be a fraud. After ten days of filming, the production shut down, and Ballycotton returned to obscurity.

The housing estate was on the right as we entered the village. The first phase was completed, but the model home was locked, I looked through every window. "This is perfect! I love it. Look at the view of the bay! I love the kitchen and the dining room and it has a perfect living room. I wonder how many bedrooms are upstairs."

Noel called the number on the window and spoke to John Brown, who turned out to be the builder. He agreed to show us the unit in an hour. We stopped in at Sean and Denise's pub to await John Brown. Sean was surprised that we were interested in the units. I tried to explain that the price was amazing, compared to real estate in America, and the view was perfect. I think I had already fallen in love with it. If Sean was skeptical, Denise was excited for us and pleased that we might be neighbors.

John showed us through the semi-detached, cement-block house, which turned out to have four bedrooms and two bathrooms upstairs, a small bathroom downstairs and a laundry room. The back garden was fenced and not too large. *Perfect,* I thought. The next phase would be ready the following May.

"Are there any units left on the front?" I asked John.

"There are two left, numbers three and five. All the rest are sold. Also you get to choose the bedroom en suites, the bathroom tiles, the kitchen cabinets, counters, and the flooring," he explained, and proceeded to list all the special things he was putting in the house. He would be on this project until completion.

Noel asked about the terms. I was leaving for America in a couple of days and wondered what we had to do to purchase that unit. John said that he would need a deposit, we would have to choose all the extras, and sign a few papers. We told him we would talk it over and call him back. As he drove away I couldn't contain my excitement.

"I love it. It's perfect! Now we'll have a place in Ireland to come home to, near family and on the water. Let's buy it."

Noel did not seem to share my enthusiasm. He was more cautious, and we bantered for more than an hour before returning to McGraths Pub for coffee and a chat with Sean and Denise. Sean remained dubious, but they could not quell my enthusiasm. The hours were slipping by, and we had to go home to change for our dinner with Ann and Bob Warren. We drove back to the housing estate and walked around the two remaining sites, looked at the view once more, and made our decision. After all, it would be another year before we would move in, and we knew the price was good compared to other sites in the area. Noel called John and said we would purchase Number 3 Silverstrand. As Noel said good-bye, I threw myself around his neck and squealed with delight.

"I can't believe it. A bedroom for each of us when the kids come to visit! And it's on the water, our dream come true. I love Ballycotton."

We arrived with our eyes sparkling for our dinner with the Warrens, who wanted to know what we had been up to as Bob handed me a glass of Chardonnay and Noel a gin and tonic.

"We bought a house!" we said in unison, laughing as Ann and Bob stared in disbelief.

"Are you kidding?" Ann said.

"No! We bought a house in Ballycotton. It's under construction and won't be finished until next year," Noel explained. "We saw it today and we will meet the agent in the morning to sign the papers."

"You never cease to amaze us. You actually bought a house, just like that. Wow, you two are a bit spontaneous."

The Warrens wanted to know all about the house and as we described it our excitement was infectious. We discussed all that we needed to do and Ann and Bob suggested various vendors. As we talked, I realized how different it is to purchase a home in Ireland: You choose the entire kitchen, from the cabinets, counters, and appliances. The bathrooms would be finished completely in tile, from floor to ceiling. There are no built-in light fixtures, just cords hanging from the ceiling. We would need to install all the towel racks, toilet paper holders, and other amenities that I was used to in an American home. In the back garden was an oil tank, our heating system. The purchase was also different: You put down a deposit and then paid in various increments as the house was built. Oh, I had much to learn.

The next two days were a blur. We met with John, signed the papers, and gave him a check for our deposit. We spoke for the rest of the morning about the countless details to be decided. We requested a garbage disposal. John would have to order that from England, as most people in Ireland do not use the device, and, as we found out later, were afraid of this new-fangled convenience. As we collaborated on our Ballycotton home, John became our constant connection, always ready to help with whatever needed to be done. After our house was finished, John was still on site, completing the other houses. We had many chats and cups of coffee over the years. He even borrowed Noel's socks once when he got soaked from the rain. John was a true Irish gentleman. His family was lovely, and we met his son and daughter, who sometimes helped him. When John was tragically killed on another of his housing sites, his death deeply affected us, as we lost a dear friend.

Before I left for California, Noel and I spent every waking minute talking about the house. When we found an item we liked, we placed the order, and left a deposit before going on to other venues. John ordered the kitchen oven, or, as they call it in Ireland, the cooker, dishwasher, refrigerator, washer and dryer from a shop in the nearby village of Cloyne. (We did not put any deposit down and the following year we stopped in the shop to pay the bill. The owner said he hadn't made up a bill as of yet, but don't worry. It was no problem; we could come back another time. I don't think that would happen anywhere else.) Looking back, it is amazing what we accomplished in a couple of days. Noel would choose the fireplace tiles—he ultimately chose a romantic art deco style that incorporated a sylphlike young woman on each side of the hearth—and a few other items returning to California in August. In between shopping we also saw friends and family for short visits. Each one, we were sure, thought we were crazy to buy a house on a whim. But we were happy with our decision, and as I packed my suitcase to go home, I was glad to know that we would have our own home in Ballycotton to return to over the years.

July. A Home in Tennessee. As expected, my kids and friends thought Noel and I were crazy to buy a house in Ireland. Back in California I was flung back into the family business and the paperwork of settling Mom's estate. Meanwhile, I awaited Noel's return in August. People kept asking when we would marry but we had been too busy to set a date. All we knew was that we wanted a simple ceremony and all the kids to be with us.

"Everyone is asking about our wedding date. Maybe we should discuss it," I suggested to Noel during one of our lengthy phone conversations. "What do you think?"

"Yes, I think we should get married." He laughed. "Remember, I asked you." "Maybe we could marry on September 22. I love that date—the day we met."

"That would be good. What do we have to do? I know Ken said he could marry us, but where?" Noel asked.

"We could get married in the backyard and have a reception somewhere else," I suggested.

"That's a great idea. What about that place in Corona del Mar that we like, the place that looks like an English cottage?"

"You mean The Five Crowns." (The restaurant is a charming half-timbered replica of The Olde Belle in Hurley on Thames in England.) "That would be perfect. I'll find out if the date is available. I can't believe we are really getting married."

"Me, too. I miss you," Noel said.

"I miss you, too. It will be great when we don't have to fly back and forth. You'll have your green card, and we can visit Ireland whenever we choose. Hey, I wonder what day of the week September twenty-second is—call you right back. Love you."

The twenty-second of September turned out to be a Sunday. I left a message for the Five Crowns' hostess. As I surveyed our unfinished backyard, I saw that we had lots to do if there was to be a wedding there any time soon. The phone interrupted my thoughts.

"Hi, Mom. Guess what?" Jeff said. "There are some town homes being built in Franklin which are a good deal."

"Tell me about it." Noel and I had been looking for another investment, though we were not going to buy pricey property in California at this time. We thought it might be a good idea to buy in Tennessee, so we would have a place of our own when we visited Jeff and Andrea.

Jeff told me about the property and planned expansion. The units were priced well and selling quickly. Jeff said he would fax me some information and guided me to the website for the area. "Maybe you want to buy a couple of them for an investment," he joked. (I could not believe we were contemplating another house—our third—this year. But we did our research and eventually paid a deposit on a two bedroom, one-and-a-half bath town home.)

I also asked Jeff about our wedding date of September 22 and learned that it was too close to Andrea's due date for airline travel. She could not fly in September.

Married!

I immediately called Noel to say that we could either move the date to August or wait until spring.

"I don't want to wait until spring," Noel replied in his calm voice. "We could get married in August, as we just want a simple ceremony. I will be there on the first, and we will be able to get a marriage license and make our plans."

I checked the kitchen calendar again. "August 30th is a Saturday. How does that date sound? Andrea could fly home before September first and then we could have all the kids here."

"Great. Hopefully that date will be open at the Five Crowns. You'd better call Ken and see if he can still marry us and make sure he gets the proper paperwork." (Under California law, anyone can perform one civil ceremony a year if the proper paperwork is filed.) "What else do we need to do? Make the guest list? I doubt anyone will come from Ireland, but I'll let them know the date."

"Wow, on August thirtieth I will be Mrs. Annie Quinn," I said with tears in my eyes. "I can hardly wait. We'll have fun planning when you get here." There was much to do, like writing our vows. This was important to Noel, as we simply could not marry in the Roman Catholic Church. When Noel grew up he was taught that if you had not married in the Catholic Church, then you were not married in the eyes of the Church. So he believed that it was OK to date me, as I was not really a divorcee. All that had changed, and the church now believed anyone married in any sort of church was indeed married. Noel had spoken to many priests and experts concerning this change. He finally spoke to a priest in Ireland, whose name I do not know, who gave him permission to marry me. Noel was told it was not a sin and he would still be allowed Communion and to be a special part of the Church. This was important to me, too, as I did not want to interfere with Noel's religious beliefs, and the Mass and Holy Communion were at his core. We could be married in a civil ceremony in our garden and hope that some day the Roman Catholic Church would bless our marriage.

"Annie, slow down," Noel said. "Let's do the planning when I get there. It should be fairly simple. Just find out about the reception. Oh, I'll also order our wedding rings from my jeweler, so don't worry about that. I love you, talk to you later."

I clicked the phone over to a dial tone, and called the kids with the date. I explained it was a second wedding for us both, and we wanted to keep it simple. A wedding at home and a nice dinner—no bouquets, no wedding cake, no frills.

Heather and Wendy disagreed. "You have to have flowers, bouquets, and a wedding cake," they said. "This is a special day and you two have to celebrate. It can be simple but you need to do some traditional things. Mom, we will order your wedding cake," Heather said in a voice that left no room for argument. "It will be simple but good. You have to have cake."

And so the planning began, plans that took on a life of their own. Amazingly, the Five Crowns had just had a wedding scheduled for the thirtieth cancelled, so the garden area was available. After Noel arrived, we got busy. We went over the menu, wine, and table seating. We formalized our list: twenty-two guests at the wedding with another thirty or so joining us at the reception. We called everyone and gave them the date. I could not choose just one bridesmaid so I chose them all: Heather, Wendy, and Andrea; my sister Lynda; and, of course, Joan and Yvette. I ordered bouquets of white roses and white hydrangeas for each to hold during the ceremony and corsages for my Aunt Dodie and my dear friend, Betty Dooley. I ordered centerpieces of roses, hydrangeas, lilies, snapdragons, and Bells of Ireland for the Five Crowns' round tables and a small floral arrangement to top the cake.

August 30. Excitement surrounded us as family and friends gathered at the house. Noel and I had snuck out to the florist and returned with the flowers, surprising everyone. Andrea did my make-up, and I dressed in a simple purple sleeveless dress with a lightweight duster jacket. Noel wore his light gray suit with a light blue shirt and no tie. Everyone gathered in the backyard as Ken presided over the simple ceremony. Gary was Noel's best man and on cue handed over the wedding band, of a simple Gaelic design, engraved with the date and our names.

"I now pronounce you man and wife. You may kiss the bride," Ken said. A cheer rose up and we were surrounded by hugs, laughter, and the click of cameras. The reception at the Five Crowns was all that we hoped for, intimate and full of joy. Jeff gave a wonderful speech welcoming Noel to the family. The food was delicious, the wine perfect, the evening calm, the conversation flowed. Heather was right about the wedding cake—it was scrumptious. Family and friends began to leave as the evening grew late, but the kids had one more surprise. As they escorted us outside, everyone had lined up in two rows, holding sparklers in an arch for Noel and me to walk through. Tears sprang to my eyes as I remembered saying to the kids, "We don't want anything for the wedding, just fireworks. I love fireworks!" They accomplished it. We ran through the arch and into a waiting car that took us to the Marriott at Fashion Island, where we spent the night. Later, after our friends left town, we would drive up the coast to Carmel.

October. Now that we were officially married, Noel applied for his green card. We had no idea how much paperwork had to be filed, documents shown, tax records proven, and letters of recommendations written. We even had to provide pictures of the two of us over the past couple of years. I understood that the government was being careful that ours was not a marriage of convenience for Noel to gain residency, but the amount of hoops we jumped through was daunting. All along the way, fees had to be paid. Apparently our relationship was suspect, as we had not filled out the paperwork for a fiancée visa, which entailed another fee. After we explained that we had planned to get married later in September but my daughter-in-law could not fly so had to move the wedding to August, the authorities were a bit appeased. Finally Noel received his temporary green card, good for three years. No more three months at a time—what a relief!

At the end of October I began filling out the paperwork to become an Irish citizen through marriage. A new law had gone in to effect, but I would be able to slip through the old rules within a certain window of time. We had to provide official documents (Mary's death certificate and my divorce decree), and more fees. The paperwork had to be exactly correct or it was sent back. We had this happen twice. We finally got the job done, and there was nothing to do but wait for the granting of my Irish citizenship.

November. Andrea's baby was due November 29. We were excited to meet our first grandchild, a boy, and decided to fly back before Thanksgiving to be there for the birth. We landed late Monday afternoon, rented a car, and drove to Jeff and Andrea's house. She was cute, so pregnant, and she and Jeff couldn't wait for the baby. We had dinner together and then settled in to our hotel, as our town home wasn't finished. In the morning we helped Jeff and Andrea pack for their move to their new house. We cleaned and sorted some of the boxes, and Andrea even began to paint one of the rooms in the new house. We made plans to see Jeff and Andrea the next morning after their early doctor's appointment. Not long now until the baby would be here.

The phone rang about 9:15 a.m.

"Mom, we're on the way to the hospital. The doctor said that the fluid around the baby is old and the baby should be delivered today," Jeff said in a voice filled with concern. "He's going to induce Andrea."

I said I had never heard of "old fluid."

"Mom, that's what he said. We're on the way now. Can you meet us there?"

Noel and I rushed to the hospital, where we were directed to Andrea and Jeff's room, a large labor suite, with a couch that pulled out to make a double bed for Jeff. Andrea was hooked up to an IV and calmly waiting for the next step. She looked so serene, yet I was sure she was terrified. Her labor began, and Jeff asked me to show Andrea how to breathe through the contractions. I helped a little, but she was finally able to get the epidural and then did not feel any pain. Her parents arrived early in the afternoon. They had hurriedly packed and driven from Sylacauga, Alabama, to be at the birth of their first grandchild. As the minutes ticked away, our excitement grew.

Jeffrey Scott Giuliano II was born on November 27, 2002. We met Scott in his pink newborn essence, the newest addition to our family. Andrea beamed, and seeing Jeff look at his son with such love and pride was a moment I will always treasure. What a year we had seen, from Mom's unexpected death to the birth of our first grandchild. The circle of life continued. Noel's and my life together was continually evolving as I became wife and Gramma in the space of a year.

Family Album

In August of 1998, my son, Jeff, and I drove Route 66 for his move to Nashville, Tennessee. Because of that old Eagles' song, "Take It Easy," of course we had to stop on "a corner in Winslow, Arizona."

September 22, 1998. With Joan, Yvette, and a traveling companion, we posed with an Irishman we had just met in the pub of the Connemara Coast Hotel. His name was Noel Quinn.

Shandon Belltower, Cork, Ireland.
Photo created by Kglavin March 2005.

In October 1998, I stopped by the Balboa
Island post office to pick up my mail,
including this mysterious envelope
postmarked "Corcaigh, Eire."

via air mail
par avion

ANN GIULIANO
P.O. BOX 5464,
BALBOA ISLAND,
CA 92662
USA.

December 1999. Noel spent his first California Christmas with me.

Noel must have been eight or nine years old in this photo taken after his release from the hospital in Coole.

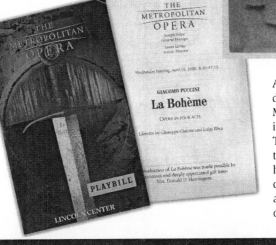

April 19, 2000. Noel's dream was to visit the Metropolitan Opera in New York City. There we experienced together the opera I had first listened to on the CD he gave me at the end of our tour of Cork.

Celebrating a moment together. 2000.

Annie's Mom and Dad, Marge and John Stonebraker.

February 13, 2001. Whenever Noel's three-month visa expired, he grew pensive. Here at Los Angeles International Airport, about to return to Ireland the day before my chemotherapy was to begin.

Three brothers Quin[n], Noel, Mick, and George, at Pamela and Derek O'Brien's wedding in Cratloe, County Clare.

Looking out together at the untamed Irish coastline.

We never tired of the views of Ballycotton Harbor.

Star of the Sea Church sits on a hill overlooking the fishing village of Ballycotton.

August 30, 2002. Wendy, the happy bride (me), and Heather after I became Mrs. Noel Quinn.

August 30, 2002. Surrounded by family and close friends in our garden just after we said our vows.

With Kay and George Quinn and Therese and Mick Quin at the Bayview Hotel, one of our favorite places to dine in Ballycotton, 2003.

Noel with his nieces, Susan, Leah, Mags, and Jean McGrath, at McGraths Pub in Ballycotton, 2003.

The St. Patrick's Day cards we sent in 2004
became a tradition, one we still celebrate.

Noel dearly loved his meanders along the Irish coastline. Here at Slea Head, on the windswept Dingle Peninsula.

Noel clowns with Scott, Johnathan, and Grant, July 2007.

May 2006. Noel was a natural as Willy Wonka. I had missed Noel's stage performances of his early twenties but got to see how he evolved into a character during the years he appeared as Willy Wonka for the children of Washington Elementary School in Santa Ana.

Thank You!!!

Mr. Willy Wonka

Ms. Morrison
Washington Elementary

Third Grade
May 2006

March 17, 2008. Celebrating St. Patrick's Day. Noel with Johnathan wearing his hat from Disneyland.

April 2008. After Noel's diagnosis, we rented a house on Balboa Island, so visiting family and friends would have plenty of room. Above: On the seawall with the grandsons.

To the right: Noel and Declan ride the Balboa Island Ferry, 2008.

April 22, 2008. All three of my children, their spouses, and my six grandsons gathered to celebrate Austin's first birthday.

September 2008. On our trips together, Noel and Gary Kilgore liked to sit and chat while the rest of us ran around sightseeing.

September 2008. My children and their families came for the Hooley and lingered to enjoy the Irish countryside.

September 2008. Noel entertained "the littles," as we called Declan, Zach, and Austin, while the rest of the family explored Barryscourt Castle in County Cork.

Noel and Austin in Barryscourt Castle garden, so typical of the joy Noel found in the boys and vice versa.

February 9, 2008. Noel holding Zachary on his first birthday,

Noel became a barber at the age of fifteen. As Granda, he took special delight in cutting the grandsons' hair. Here, with Grant.

September 2008. One afternoon Noel fished from the pier in Ballycotton Bay.

I donated a tree in Noel's memory to the Peter and Mary Muth Interpretive Center on Newport's Back Bay. We often took the boys to the Science Center there. The tree, dubbed "the Granda Tree," was dedicated with all seven grandsons present in March 2011.

We loved traveling with the Bovards and the Kilgores. Here Joan and Ken Bovard (left) and Gary and Yvette Kilgore on our way to Denali National Park in Alaska.

May 2012. Chrystal and Ben Copenhaver, with baby Emmalyn, at their graduation from Shepherdstown College. To Chrystal, Noel was the grandfather she never had.

Brady Christopher Carey, our seventh grandson, was born on December 27, 2010.

Romance, Continued

The American Family Comes to Ireland

ecember 28, 2003. Noel and I could hardly wait for Andrea, Jeff, and Scott to clear customs at Shannon Airport. Soon Heather and Derek and Wendy and Andy would arrive at the airport in Cork. Their visit would allow everyone to meet Noel's family, see our home in Ballycotton, and experience our Irish life. After we bought our Ballycotton house, people often wondered why we need four bedrooms. "So all the kids will have their own rooms when they visit," I would explain, though never expecting that we would ever have a full house. Now they were all coming to Ireland—wow!

Noel had rented a large van to hold the nine of us. I always kidded him that after meeting me he had taken on several new roles as chauffer, driving vehicles much larger than he had ever needed in the past, as tour guide, and as general liaison between America and Ireland.

We all spent a lovely week or so in the Ballycotton area. Although it was winter and cold, the kids bundled up and explored Main Street.

McGraths Pub was just a block away, and we spent time at Denise and Sean's upstairs apartment, where Scott and their two-year-old granddaughter, Leah, had great fun playing together. We also paused at Stephen Pearce's pub, who had optimistically set up in business when the Marlon Brando film *Divine Rapture* had looked like a sure thing. When it turned out that the film was not a sure thing, Pearce had installed a gravestone, since removed, outside the pub:

RIP

Divine Rapture

B. 10th July 1995

D. 23rd July 1995

We walked the beaches, and hiked a bit of the famous though damp and slippery Ballycotton Cliff Walk. We had fun at the house, too, playing board games, cooking, and settling into Irish life. With Noel driving—I never felt confident driving on the unfamiliar side of the road—we traveled the back roads to visit the marvelous Cobh Museum, filled with local lore about Irish emigration, the *Titanic's* last port of call, and the torpedoing of the *Lusitania* by a German U-boat off the coast in 1915. The kids enjoyed the Jameson Distillery in nearby Midleton, and we visited Blarney Castle. While my family walked the spiral staircase to kiss the Blarney Stone, Noel and I remained in the van. There, Noel entertained fourteen-month-old Scott with the steering wheel, blinkers, and dashboard gadgets for more than an hour.

We toured County Cork and met more of Mary's family: her brother, Michael McGrath, and his wife, Sheila, at their dairy farm in Ballyrobin, where we enjoyed her homemade brown bread and blackberry jam together in the kitchen, and stomped through their fields to meet their cows, up close and personal. In Ballyadreen we visited Mary's brother, Phil McGrath, and his wife, Kay, at their lovely home next to the original McGrath home, with its breathtaking view of the Atlantic Ocean.

One day, as we drove in the cumbersome van to see Mick and Therese Quin, Noel explained why their last name is spelled with one "n." When Mick was born, his aunt registered the birth, spelling his last name with one "n" as had a grandfather years ago. George and Noel, however, have two "n"s in their last name, as the family never allowed that aunt to register any more births. So within the family, Mick is a "Quin," and George and Noel are "Quinn."

Therese was smitten with Scott. Scott would hold his hands high over his head whenever someone asked, "How big is Scott?" Therese loved this and giggled each time he performed his trick. (After all these years, Therese still says, "How big is Scott?" and we are all taken back to that moment.) Mick uncorked a bottle of champagne, and there was much excitement when we learned that Therese had a big surprise for us. She had contacted the Lord Mayor of Cork, much to Noel's chagrin, as he never liked attention drawn to him, and we were to visit City Hall. When the limousine arrived, though, there was no car seat for Scott, the rules on such things being different in Ireland. Instead we held Scott close as we made the short journey. The Lord Mayor was unavailable, but his assistant welcomed us into the chambers and asked each of us to sign the official book of Cork City. We took a family photo, which later appeared in the Cork *Examiner*. Afterward, Mick and Therese hosted a wonderful lunch at the nearby Imperial Palace Hotel.

Noel and I had planned a party, too, to officially introduce his entire Irish family to their new American family. We traveled to the Bunratty Castle Hotel in County Clare for the night. The upstairs room at the Creamery restaurant was a perfect venue. We had encouraged Noel's family to bring everyone, young and old—no need for a babysitter— and mixed the seating arrangements so the Americans and Irish would mingle. As I have said, the party piece was such a special part of the Irish tradition, and I was delighted to see my family experience it. I still remember Heather's encounter in the loo with Noel's great-niece, Niamh, who, at age twelve or thirteen, had just sung, a capella, "Somewhere Over the Rainbow."

"I'm so impressed that you sang a song by yourself at a party," Heather said to her.

"Oh, well, what do you do at your parties in America?" replied Niamh.

Heather was left to wonder what we actually do at our American parties.

The evening was a success. The families got to know each other, shared stories, sang party pieces, and began new friendships that flowered over the years. That night we had a photo taken of our family, which we later included in a St. Patrick's Day card sent to people around the world. The card would become an annual tradition.

January 14, 2004. It was time to return to America. Heather and Derek would stay on for a few days in

Ballycotton, where they would relax and explore more areas of the countryside. Mick and Therese would pick them up later in the week and take them to Cork Airport for their return flight. As we departed from Ireland, Noel and I held hands and spoke about the wonder of sharing our families. My children had experienced the Irish countryside and the kindness of Noel's fun-loving family and friends. They could now visualize all the places and people I had spoken of, and I hoped they better understood how I fell in love with Ireland, and with Noel.

* * * * *

Noel brought richness to my family in so many ways. In 2004, Wendy was student teaching in Lindsey Deems' third grade class at Washington Elementary School in Santa Ana, California. It came time to cast the class play, *Willy Wonka & the Chocolate Factory.* Others had played the role of Willy Wonka, and the year before Mrs. Deems herself had played the part. Now Mrs. Deems decided to look for a new star. Wendy naturally thought of Noel. Actually, she volunteered him, explaining to Mrs. Deems that Noel had a theatrical background. Wendy called, and after Noel got over his amazement, said that he would be happy to play the part, although he had never seen the film. I rented the movie and enjoyed it all over again as we watched Gene Wilder play the wild and crazy Willy Wonka. Noel loved it.

The class read the book and then wrote to "Mr. Wonka" with an invitation to visit their classroom. In return, he sent golden tickets to a few of the children who had been chosen by the teacher to help out should he appear.

One fine day, Willy Wonka appeared unexpectedly at Mrs. Deems' classroom. In his red blazer, black pants, white shirt, top hat, cane (made from a blackthorn bush by his friend in Ireland), and an Irish accent, Noel was perfect in the role. He had also brought along a chocolate fountain to dip marshmallows in, made chocolate pudding, and handed out Gobstoppers from his "factory."

The experience was a success, and for a couple of years Noel was invited back for encore performances. The kids were always so excited when he walked through their door. Full of questions about the characters in the book, from Violet to Charlie, they wanted to know about the Oompa-Loompas, Grandpa Joe, and whether Willy was married. Afterwards we were surprised when they asked for his autograph. Noel patiently signed "Willy Wonka" for all the kids.

I loved watching Noel play this role. He was a natural actor and one could easily believe he was Willy. The teachers were thrilled, and the kids wrote thank-you letters, which were incorporated into a booklet with "Willy Wonka" on the cover.

During 2004 we also had the privilege of hosting Noel's great nieces from Shannon. Aoife, fourteen years old and Niamh, thirteen years old, came for a three-week visit. We had so much fun showing the girls Southern California, from Disneyland and Hollywood to the local beaches. They loved musicals and often we would sit at home and watch *Oklahoma*, *The King and I*, and *Fiddler on the Roof*. We also took them to an Angels baseball game, had barbecues, and spent time wandering the shops of Fashion Island and

South Coast Plaza. We had other visitors from Ireland, too, like Noel's niece, Sue Curley and her husband, John, our friends, Maura and Don Kelly, and Noel's brother Mick and his wife, Therese. Each of these visits was special and Noel loved to show off the area and the reasons why he loved living in Orange County and California.

Granda

Noel loved to be called Granda. Although he had no biological children, my three children embraced him and, when their own children were born, wanted him called "Granda," not just Noel. He was, at first, surprised and then humbled by the honor.

When our first grandson, Jeffrey Scott Giuliano, arrived, Noel and I had watched in awe as Scott was cleaned up, weighed, and measured. I realized we were experiencing grandparenthood together, with no baggage or expectations. Noel just got to skip those hectic years of parenthood. At first, I did not realize how much fun it would be to take on this new role with Noel, who always seemed to have the touch to get a crying baby to sleep.

Two years later we were blessed with two more grandchildren. Grant Davis Giuliano was born on June 17, 2004, in Nashville. Again, we were able to be at the hospital for Grant's birth. Along with Andrea's parents, we entertained Scott, while Jeff stayed by his wife's side in the delivery room. It was magical all over again to watch Jeff with his dark-haired, brown-eyed baby in the nursery, and to watch Scott marvel at his new brother.

On October 8, 2004, Noel and I joined family and friends at Hoag Hospital in Newport Beach, eager to find out what Wendy was having, as she and Andy had chosen not to learn the baby's gender in advance. When Andy appeared, he told us the news: Johnathan Andrew Carey had arrived. As everyone crowded around Johnathan in the nursery, I slipped into the recovery room to see Wendy. She had been taken to the delivery room quickly, as her blood pressure skyrocketed, and had a Caesarian section, and I wanted to make sure she was all right. Meanwhile Noel watched, just as proud and fascinated as the other two grandfathers, while Johnathan was washed, weighed, and measured.

In 2007 we were blessed with a trifecta of grandchildren. Heather, Andrea, and Wendy were all pregnant and would deliver within three months of one another. Like Wendy and Andy, Heather and Derek did not want to know their baby's gender in advance, so when we gathered on January 29 at Hoag Hospital, the anticipation in the waiting room was high. Then Derek walked out and held up a blue belt. Declan Burton Anderson had arrived. Heather had a C-section, so we had to wait until she and Declan were settled in a room. Finally I was able to hold Declan just before his first bath. With this fourth grandchild to welcome to the world, none of the magic of birth had left us. Noel and I found him as unique as the other three.

Jeff and Andrea had told us there was no need to come to Tennessee for the birth of their third son, as they would need our help later in the month. But Noel and I could not let an opportunity pass to greet each grandchild at his birth. We arrived in Nashville on February eighth, as Andrea was to be induced the next morning and stayed near the hospital. We did not tell Jeff we were in town. When Noel and I arrived at the door to their room, it was closed. We knocked. They called, "Come in," but we did not open the door. They said it again, and we knocked again. When Jeff finally opened the door, he was shocked to see us standing there.

Zachary Quinn Giuliano arrived on February ninth. Scott and Grant came to the hospital to see their new brother, and we all watched as he was weighed, measured, and washed. Another unique and special little boy had entered our life. Noel was thrilled to learn that Jeff and Andrea had honored him by giving Zachary the middle name of Quinn.

On April twenty-second we gathered again at Hoag Hospital to await the arrival of Wendy and Andy's baby. Surely our streak of grandsons had to end. When Andy came out of the delivery room, he teased us with pictures of the baby as we tried to guess the gender. We had been blessed with another unique little boy, Austin James Carey. Johnathan got to watch his new brother behind the nursery window.

We now had *six* grandsons, each with a special personality. We loved each of them and treasured their visits. Noel let them help out in the garden, sharing his knowledge of plant life and always quietly talking and reassuring, whether they were pulling weeds, picking flowers, or playing in the fountain. After the garden chores were done, he would relax on the patio while the boys rode their big wheels and scooters around his chair. Whenever Johnathan came for a sleepover, which was often, we lit the candles on the dining table and Noel taught him, as well as Scott and Grant, to use the candlesnuffer to extinguish the flames. At dinner Noel played a game called "make the peas disappear." I would get a small spoonful of vegetables, usually peas, to encourage the boys to eat their greens. Noel, with a wink to the boys, would tell me to turn around, as there was something behind me. When I turned my head, keeping the spoonful of peas suspended, the grandson would sneak the spoonful of peas into his mouth, with a giggle. I would turn back to them, shocked to see that the peas had disappeared, and would quickly ask, "What happened to the peas?" Noel and his small co-conspirator would innocently shrug their shoulders. We would repeat the game several times, and always, to the delight of our grandsons, Gramma was tricked again. Noel loved dinner conversation and helped me to instill in each of the boys, no matter how young, the importance of family dining time. We always turned off the television and shared ideas, the day's events, and funny stories. Noel also valued good manners and encouraged the boys to say "please" and "thank you," leading by example by saying, "Thank you, Gramma, for our dinner."

Noel showed the boys the world of nature, too. He liked to drive them in our golf cart, *Silly Bug,* along Back Bay Drive to watch for wildlife: rabbits, egrets, crabs. We liked to watch the baby ospreys in their nest by Shellmaker Island and feel the wonder of the natural world. Often we let the boys touch the prickles of the cactus, blow the dandelions' white fluff, collect shells and rocks, and play along the shore. We also watched for different shapes of clouds as they drifted by. The Peter and Mary Muth Interpretive Center on University Drive on the Back Bay was one of our favorite hangouts. Through its excellent ranger program and learning classroom, the boys were able to watch snakes slither behind their glass enclosures, frogs balance on rocks in a funny type of tide pool, and stingrays, starfish and various other fish. The classroom was filled with puzzles, puppets, crafts and fun. Ranger Sue, who became a good friend, led a program for two- to eight-year olds. Each time the theme was different, and the boys loved it. She would read a story, do a craft, and lead a hike. Noel liked to follow the boys as they explored, often as intrigued and excited as they were. Because of his patience, the boys were free to explore and develop their love of nature in a safe environment.

Our walks around Balboa Island and rides on the Balboa Ferry (once traveling back and forth on the same ferry four times) always felt like an adventure, as we searched for sea life and bugs, and took great delight whenever we spotted a seal barking in the harbor. And when we took all the boys to Ireland, Noel continued to show them the great outdoors, from Willy Wagtail, the bird, to the wonderful Fota Wildlife Park on an island near Carrigtohill in County Cork, where animals roam free. Noel always had a camera around his neck and took countless pictures of animals, flowers, and impromptu shots of the boys as they discovered bugs, snails, and special treasures to put in their pockets.

The boys, as we called them, were a joy. Although he had been active in the lives of his nieces and nephews as they grew up, it was nothing like being a fulltime hands-on Granda to these little boys. He served as the boys' barber, and taught them sit still, whether in their walker, high chair, or on Gramma's lap, while he cut their hair. This was a special time for him, as he talked softly to each of them. They trusted him and seldom fussed as the scissors, never clippers, moved close to their ears.

With each year our Easter egg hunt had become a great competition between Noel and the kids—especially the grown kids, as they were never able to find all the eggs hidden in the garden. Months later a plastic egg would appear in the shed or fall on the ground out of a bush, and Noel took great glee in calling the kids and to inform them, "We found another egg!"

After the grandsons were old enough to take part, Noel's famous Easter egg hunt took on another dimension. The first year we had a grandchild in the hunt Noel had put some eggs on the ground within easy access of Johnathan's chubby little hands. However the grown-up "boys" swooped up every egg in sight—oh, the competition was fierce. But the Easter egg hunt and Granda's special hiding places became interwoven into our family traditions.

The boys loved our Fourth of July celebrations because they were able to help decorate *Silly Bug* and their bikes or scooters, march in a parade, swim, enjoy a barbecue and hot fudge sundaes, and watch the fireworks. Noel dove happily into the festivities, helping with all the aspects of this uniquely American holiday. He drove the kids in the golf cart, helped me buy all the party supplies. As the fireworks boomed overhead, I would look over at Noel and often see him holding a sleeping boy on his lap.

Noel passed on his love of music. He made sure each of the grandsons had a *bodhrán*, a traditional Celtic drum of goatskin, a tin whistle, and a recorder. He liked to do impromptu drum sessions with sticks and logs. Our house was always filled with music, from opera to classical to jazz. Noel had been trained to sing opera but he could also sing quiet Irish ballads to the boys in his incredible voice. Whenever he sang such a ballad, "Molly Malone," for example, instead of his party piece, he encouraged the boys to sing along.

As Granda, Noel drew on his training in Irish community theater. He was a fine actor with a strong reading voice. He mesmerized the boys whenever he read, "Going on a Bear Hunt," holding their attention by softly leading them to the end with 'Tip toe, tip toe ... and then, loudly, "A BEAR!" Each time the boys shrieked with fright and laughter. Time spent on Granda's lap reading was a special time for each of the boys, when he gave them his full attention.

One of Noel's greatest joys was his grandsons. He took pride in watching the boys develop and always made time for them. He loved the quiet moments in which he could share his wisdom with them. He had a calming presence, whether with a kind look, a soft reassurance, a time to read, or listening to music. Being Granda was a special honor for Noel, and I do believe all of the boys were lucky to have such a special man in their lives.

Traveling the World Together

During Noel's first visit to California and my visit later in 1999 to Ireland, we had rediscovered our individual worlds through one another's eyes. On those trips we had fallen in love. We had also fallen into an easy rhythm on the road. Before we met, I had traveled throughout the United States, Canada, Mexico, and Europe. I thought I had seen plenty of the world. Now, with Noel, I found a renewed pleasure in travel. We loved meeting the locals and liked to avoid well-traveled highways and tourist attractions. We would listen to music, stop at small towns, laugh, talk, and pause to take just one more photo. Each journey, even a simple road trip, became a new adventure.

I think I expanded Noel's horizons, too, sometimes pushing him to new experiences and roles, like his serving as tour guide/van driver. In 1999, we had shown Yvette and Gary around the Ireland Noel knew so well. Yvette and I had thought it was a great idea. Noel, of course, knew Yvette from our first encounter in Connemara, and this would be his first meeting with Gary. But as we approached the Kilgores' hotel room in Dublin, I had doubts: *Annie, what were you thinking? Gary is a good friend of Jim's.*

What if he doesn't like Noel? And we're going to be in a small car together for how many days?

Then the door opened, Gary extended his hand in welcome, and the two men became instant friends. As they later liked to say, they had been friends for forty-seven years. On this trip, we meandered through small villages to shop, took pictures of every castle we saw, let Yvette photograph every sheep or lamb she found, and just enjoyed one another's company. Amazingly Noel's car, Volkswagen Golf, was able to hold the four of us, our luggage, and all the packages we acquired as we traversed the countryside.

We had so much fun together that we planned another visit to Ireland, Scotland, Wales, and Northern Ireland the following September, this time with the Bovards. Gary was of Scottish heritage and had always wanted to visit his homeland. Noel decided to lease a van in Cork and drive us through Ireland, and then ferry over the Irish Sea to Wales and Scotland. He asked everyone what they wanted to see and figured out the routes we would take within the time available. Noel was a great sport in all of this, as he was used to driving small European cars. Now he was the chauffeur in charge of an economy van to haul these American tourists around the countryside. We even had navy blue sweatshirts made up for each of the couples that read "Quinn's International Tours" on the back; Noel's read "Tour Guide" on the front. Again we had a wonderful time, seeing villages, coastlines, pubs, castles, and ancient battlegrounds. At one point, though, the hatch blew off the van into the water as we crossed a bridge over the wonderfully named Firth of Forth, in Scotland. We found a small shop where the local tradesmen fashioned a repair, would not let us pay, and sent us on our merry way within a couple of hours. We were amazed, as the Scots are known for their thrift. Only once during that trip, did Noel feel really uncomfortable. That was in Northern Ireland because we were driving through various villages with "CORK" emblazoned on the side of the van. He felt it too conspicuous and hoped it would not lead to any trouble with the opposing political and military factions that had fought so bitterly for decades.

Our travels took us around the world. We showed up at the weddings of Noel's various nieces and nephews, both Quinns and McGraths. He was still "Uncle Noel," dearly loved by all the family and children. Our visit to the wedding of Noel's nephew, Paul McGrath (Sean and Denise's son), in Sydney, Australia, was a highlight. We had invited the Bovards to go with us and planned to visit the North Island of New Zealand beforehand. Noel was a big hit on our visit there, becoming the official Maori warrior from our group. He wore the necklace and learned the face of the Maori, with its grimaces and wagging tongue. We loved the coastline, small towns, and the leisurely pace and friendliness of the New Zealanders. We left reluctantly, with plans to return someday to the South Island.

The rainy weather in Sydney did not stop us from enjoying the sights: the Opera House, the zoo, the blue mountains, and the harbor. Paul and Jenny had a lovely church ceremony followed by a yummy reception in the Royal Botanic Gardens. There we became fascinated with the large fruit bats hanging from the trees, who suddenly took flight as the sun set. (The bats, however, known as the grey-headed flying foxes, were seen as a pest by locals. Suspected of killing many of the trees in the park, the colony of 22,000 bats was later relocated.)

Paul is an accomplished chef—he and Jenny own and operate The Ortolan restaurant on Bayswater—and Paul's colleagues business provided a marvelous array of their specialties, from great platters of oysters, shrimp, and mussels, to dainty Chinese dumplings and meat-filled savory spices. We felt welcomed to Sydney as friends, rather than tourists.

Another of Noel's nephews by his first marriage, Stephen Crowe, married in Seattle in August 2004. Since none of Mary's family in the United Kingdom could attend, Noel represented Stephen's family. We had a wonderful time with Stephen's mum, Dymphna, Mary's youngest sister. We went to Pike's Market and explored the city of Seattle. At lunch Noel met my uncle, Brother Michael Stonebraker, a retired Episcopal monk from the Order of the Holy Cross. I was happy that they got to meet, for they enjoyed one another's conversation. The wedding was small and memorable, with a couple of moments of that weekend still locked in my memory. When we first spoke on the phone with the bride-to-be, Melanie, she had jokingly asked, "How will I know you, Uncle Noel?" He responded that he would be wearing a silly hat, not really expecting to show up in one. One afternoon, while Noel took his afternoon nap, Dymphna and I visited Pike's Market, where we found a magnificent balloon hat displayed in one of the stalls. I asked the proprietor the price but she refused the inquiry, saying, "It is not for sale. I had the balloon man make it earlier in the day."

I pleaded, explaining our urgent need for just this silly hat. She relented, and Dymphna and I carried that balloon hat back to our hotel. Noel, of course, thought it was magical and happily wore it to meet Melanie.

My second memory of that weekend occurred the next day. We had taken Dymphna sightseeing in the San Juan Islands. We lost track of time, missed an earlier ferry, and had just enough time to get Dymphna to the wedding venue for pictures. To do this, she had to dress for the wedding in the ferryboat's head. We giggled as she changed, combed her hair, and discovered another person also dressing for a wedding in the head. At the wedding Noel gave an eloquent speech to the couple. Dymphna traveled home with us, where we spent a wonderful week sharing Newport Beach with her.

Many other nieces and nephews married in Ireland and we went to various weddings from Ballycotton to Shannon and throughout the country. One of the first weddings I attended was Pamela and Derek's. The Kilgores attended the wedding, too, and Gary joked that he was their "Uncle Gary" from America—it is always a big deal in Ireland when a relative returns for a visit from America.

Irish weddings operated differently from those in the U.S. Yvette and I wanted to go to the church a bit early to see the set up. Pamela Quinn and Derek O'Brien's wedding was scheduled for four o'clock, but Noel said no one would be there at four—it being an Irish wedding, that meant four-*ish*, Irish time. (Since most Irish churches do not offer facilities to dress and prepare for the wedding, the wedding party usually dresses at home.) Yvette and I did not believe him and insisted going to the church early. But as we drove up into the empty parking lot, we realized Noel was right; no one was there. As we wandered inside, the priest walked up and laughingly said, "Boy, you must have wanted a good seat." The guests began arriving around three forty-five, with many of the women wearing hats or fascinators (small hair adornments, usually of feathers, flowers, or beads), but no one entered the church. Instead they milled around outside, awaiting the bride's arrival. The bridal party arrived around four-fifteen-*ish,* and then the guests filed into the church, followed by the groomsmen who sat in the front pews with the groom. The bridesmaids walked quickly down the aisle and sat in the front pews, followed by Pamela and her father, George. The wedding was lovely and after Mass the bride and groom sat at a table and signed the church registry. The reception began with tea and cookies in the hotel foyer, while some of the men gravitated to the adjoining pub for toasts before the official reception began.

Although all of our trips had a sense of fun and wonder, I think our cruise to Alaska in 2006 ranks near the top. With Yvette and Gary and Joan and Ken as our companions once again, we embarked at Vancouver, British Columbia. Each couple had verandah suites so as to enjoy the views of the glaciers, coastline and sea life. Although it was cold Noel would put on his jacket, throw a camera around his neck, and stand enthralled by the scenery, especially Glacier Bay. The six of us had great fun viewing the

Inside Passage, exploring Ketchikan and Juneau, playing games of Sequence, and enjoying the nightly shows and dinners. We had extended our trip to include a train trip from Anchorage to Fairbanks, with a stopover in Denali Park, another highlight of our trip, where we saw moose, grizzly bears with their cubs, and eagles soaring overhead, as we drove through the park in a run-down bus. On our first day in the park we could not see Denali's majestic peak until we were about sixteen miles into the park. The next day, however, was magnificent, without a cloud in the sky, and Denali Peak was visible to all within the park. The Kilgores had booked a six-seater plane and invited us to join them. We looked for the Bovards to see if they wanted to go but could not find them. (We later learned they had taken a hike.) Noel was like a kid in a candy shop, snapping photo after photo with every twist and turn of the small plane, trying to capture the beauty of the crystalline blue sky against the stark, snow-covered peaks. The small plane was dwarfed by the magnificence of the scenery, the vastness of the snow, and the sheer drama of the cliffs.

We made plans to cruise the Panama Canal. Noel had always wanted to see the construction of the magnificent canal as well as something of Central America. But when we learned we were expecting another grandchild in April, we postponed the trip. Noel dreamed of other trips, too, like a cruise from Valparaiso to Buenos Aires, a drive through the Bordeaux region of France, a train trip in the Canadian Rockies, and, especially, a visit to Italy for the opera. He told me he used to ask his clients to send postcards whenever they traveled, which he pinned to the walls of his barbershop. These postcards were reminders of the world beyond Ireland, and I think his imagination, well cultivated during his years in the hospital as a boy, freed him to visualize and learn about the rest of world.

As Noel and I wandered the world, my shell collection grew. In New Zealand I found a sunshine yellow shell and in Australia an azure shell with blue and black spots. Canada offered up a unique oyster shell. In Ballycotton one finds shells that look like Chinese coolie hats, and on the North Carolina coast are a plethora of the common nutmeg and false angel-wing shells. Balboa Island has lots of clam, mussel and spiral-shaped shells; Santa Catalina Island has the wonderful abalone, with its iridescent interior. (You can tell how old an abalone is by counting the holes in its shell.) And everywhere we picked up sea glass, bits of old bottles in various colors, worn and smoothed by the ocean's natural rock tumbler.

In late May of 2007, Noel and I planned to attend the high school graduation in Maryland of my former student, Chrystal. We decided to leave early and take in the sights of our nation's Capitol. Over four days, we explored the city on foot and by car. We were only able to view the outside of the White House, as we were not quick enough to get advance tickets, but we visited the Capitol and walked around the Lincoln Memorial, the Viet Nam Memorial, and the Washington Monument, where we cooled our feet in the reflecting pool. We also tried to wander as much of the Smithsonian Institution as possible, from the famous Castle, dating to 1847, to the National Museum of American History—so much to see yet so little time. The weather was perfect, although there was quite a bit of smog in the air, which surprised me, given the city's location on the banks of the Potomac. At the John F. Kennedy Center for the Performing Arts we attended the Neil Simon play, *They're Playing Our Song*, starring Lucie Arnez, Robert Klein, and Marvin Hamlisch. (The play ran for only three nights, so we were lucky to find seats in this beautiful and historical theater.) Seeing a live Neil Simon play brought back memories of our first meeting in that Connemara pub, when Noel had been reading *Neil Simon Rewrites: A Memoir*. Now here we were, nine years later, experiencing Simon's play together.

We also visited Arlington National Cemetery. My Dad's father, a Navy veteran of World War I, is buried there, but when I asked at the front desk for the location of his grave I was told they needed to know the year of his death in order to locate it. I guessed at 1951 but was wrong, so we simply joined the tour. I had been to Arlington twice before, once as a fifteen-year-old and then in the 1980's with my children. In those years we had easy access to the entire cemetery and drove around at our leisure. After 911 and the advent of Homeland Security, however, people had to be bussed in, unless they had relatives buried in the cemetery. The tour was informative and the Tomb of the Unknown Soldier was as impressive as ever. As I looked out over all the simply marked graves, I wished I could see my grandfather's marker. When we returned to the tour center, I guessed a couple of other possible years of his death. It turned out that 1954 was the correct year; they handed me a pass that enabled us to drive to the grave marked, "George Garrigus Stonebraker," not far from John F. Kennedy's eternal flame. We then meandered the cemetery, which is sectioned off by wars, from the Civil War to the present Iraq and Afghanistan conflicts. *What a waste,* I thought. *All those young lives lost.*

Then we drove to Hagerstown, Maryland, for Chrystal's graduation from St. Maria Goretti's High School. I was introduced as Chrystal's fairy godmother, and Noel was assumed to be her Granda, which he was. She had made lots of friends. She had participated in extracurricular activities, from softball to the Junior Fireman program. As I watched my fairy goddaughter join the processional, I could not help but reflect how wonderful it was that this young woman had made it out of the crazy child welfare system. Her grades were good; she was headed for college. Chrystal was going to be all right.

A Return to Coole

2008. Early in February we flew to Ireland for the wedding of Noel's great-nephew, David Scanlon, at the Killashee House Hotel, in Naas town, County Kildare. The hotel is a quaint manor, surrounded by 200 acres of gardens, with views of the Wicklow Mountains. Although the weather was deemed dreadful by all the weathermen and locals, Noel and I found it refreshingly tranquil, with snow dusting the usually green countryside. David and Sinead's wedding was untraditional but elegant and meaningful. Noel and I held hands as they exchanged vows, and I thought back to our own untraditional wedding in the garden of our house, both days filled with joy, happiness, and love.

The reception was held in the hotel's large banquet room, filled with flickering candlelight and elaborate centerpieces of white lilies and roses. The murmur of family and friends warmed the room, such a contrast from the snow-laden pathways outside the hotel. We sat with Noel's sister Lilian and her husband, Jerry Scanlon, the groom's grandparents, and other of Noel's nieces and nephews. Music played softly as the guests dined on steak or fish, accompanied by the traditional Irish vegetable and potato, and sipped Cabernet Sauvignon or Chardonnay. The conversation ranged from vacations to politics, and I again realized that the art of Irish conversation, so different from that of America, is of a non-materialistic persuasion. The Irish, as do most Europeans, do not value their self-worth by their job but by their spirit, ideas, and diversified interests. They love to banter over politics and ideology, exchanging their various opinions without shouting, and leaving as friends at the end of the evening.

After dinner, the dancing began, from modern-day jive to slow dances, fox trots, and waltzes, and, of course, traditional Irish folk dancing, where everyone joined in, young and old. Later, we wandered into the sitting rooms for an after-dinner drink and further conversation. Somehow Noel's lengthy hospitalization as a child came up. One of his nephews, Paul or Greg, asked where the hospital was located.

Noel replied that it was in Coole, a village near Dublin.

"Have you ever been back?"

"No, that was over sixty years ago, and I'm sure the hospital is gone, as it was made of wood and canvas," Noel said. But the conversation had piqued his curiosity.

"Maybe we could drive through Coole on the way to Dublin Airport tomorrow," Noel said as we returned to our room. We had left the day open to explore the countryside—plenty of time to find Coole.

"Do you know where it is?" I asked.

"Not exactly. It isn't too far from Dublin. I do wonder after all these years what happened to it."

I found it amazing that Noel had never returned to the hospital where he spent much of his childhood. He often said that time was just a small part of his life and never really wondered about it, at least until I began asking lots of questions.

The following morning Noel located Coole, a village of several hundred people in the Irish midlands, on the map and got specific directions from the concierge. It was a beautiful day, with intermittent rain but luckily no snow, as we drove along the N-55 before turning west. Rainsqualls trailed us as we drove the narrow curving roads. I was surprised that Coole was so far from the city, almost an hour's drive from Dublin, as Noel had always remembered that fateful boyhood car trip as brief.

Suddenly Noel said, "This stretch of road seems familiar. I remember a dip in the road and that long sloping hill to the field where they would push our beds on warm days."

Noel had seen this road only twice, driving to the hospital, and, five years later, driving home; yet he remembered. He made a U-turn and drove into a small shopping complex with a pharmacy.

"Why don't you go in and ask the chemist?" I prompted.

"I don't think they will know anything, as it happened so long ago."

"Oh, Noel, since we are here, just ask."

No matter where you are in the world, men do not like to ask for directions. But he went inside and asked a young clerk if she knew where the old orthopedic hospital had been.

"The clerk nodded toward the window at a fenced construction area. That's what they are tearing down. You should ask one of the workmen."

Noel came out of the pharmacy with a big smile. "I was right. This is the place."

We returned to the construction area, where Noel explained to the man at the gate that he had been in this hospital in 1942. The man seemed a bit surprised. He told us that the building being demolished had been built, with walls and modern conveniences, in the late 1950s. It had replaced the old hospital made of canvas walls and wood that Noel had known. Originally known as "The Cripples Home," its proper name was St. Joseph's Orthopaedic Hospital.

"Would you like to come inside and walk around? Just be careful of all the debris."

With that, the foreman swung open the gate, and we entered the place where Noel had spent five years of his childhood. We looked into some of the rooms still standing, and then wandered outside to the muddy field. Noel stood quietly as memories washed over him.

"I remember being so happy when our beds were pushed out and we could see the sky and the clouds drift by. Although we couldn't get up we felt free with the sun on our faces, the birds chirping, and fresh air blowing our sheets, " he said.

"How often did you get to come to the field?" I asked, as my mind envisioned beds pushed one by one over the muddy, uneven ground.

"Not very often. It had to be a sun-filled day with no chance of rain. It was hard for the beds to be pushed out. They couldn't take a chance of bad weather as they couldn't push the beds back in quickly. Oh, how I loved those days! I still like to be out in the sunshine and have loads of windows around to look outside."

Walking with Noel in the field that day, I tried to absorb the impact of his ordeal. Every doctor we ever saw in

America had been shocked by this story. And I remained amazed that he remembered only the positive happy times of his hospital stay. Everything about him that I had fallen in love with, from his calm understanding to his acceptance of any situation, had to be linked somehow to this period in his life. His ability to chat for hours and to sit in complete stillness, as he liked to do, had to originate from his time of being tied to the bed. Noel held no bitterness and expressed love for his caregivers, from the nuns to the doctors. He often spoke of the other boys nearby, never really seeing them nor knowing their ailments, or recalling any of their names, but remembering the great fun and laughter they had through their chats, their mighty *craic*. Perhaps that is why wealth and status never impressed him, and he always treated people in the same manner, as human beings. Whenever he gave money to the poor, he always looked them in the eye and shook their hands, offering them the respect and dignity of any other person. Noel truly believed we were all equals. He dearly loved the Roman Catholic Mass, instilled at home as a young child and reinforced here by his new family of nuns. Noel lived his religion daily, believing in it deeply, though never preaching it. His life simply reflected his beliefs, morals, and values. It was a great gift that we had found the hospital site, where Noel was able to see where he lived more than sixty years ago. I felt fortunate to recall with him that home of nuns with angelic hats and canvas walls that rolled up, where a little boy, strapped to a bed by who knows what, never getting up or sitting up, learned how to read and write in his bed, among his new "brothers" and friends—and always joyful when they were rolled out into this field to watch the sun and the clouds drift by.

As we drove away from Coole, I think Noel felt a sense of relief to have visited this place. We hurried on to Dublin, anxious to plan our next adventure, a cruise through the Panama Canal.

Diagnosis

March 13, 2008. I had just arrived at Wendy's house in Orange for a girls' night out—a Pampered Chef party, when the phone rang.

"It's Noel, Mom. He wants to talk to you."

I was surprised, as we had just said good-bye. I glanced at my watch: 6:25, and took the phone.

"Dr. Pan just called with my blood test results," Noel said in a strained voice. "He wants to see us first thing in the morning. He said it's serious."

"He just called? This late in the day? What else did he say?"

"Nothing, just come in first thing," Noel said in a voice I had not heard before.

"I'll be right home."

"No, just stay and enjoy your party. I'll be all right."

"I'm coming home." I quickly explained to my daughters that Dr. Pan had recently ordered a routine blood test for Noel's cholesterol and the report had come back with something wrong. We would meet with the doctor in the morning. Noel had sounded upset, so I was going home.

"Oh, no," Heather and Wendy said in unison, as sisters often do.

"Sorry for tonight," I said, as I hugged them both and hurried to my car.

As I sped down the 55 Freeway, my mind jumped to a million conclusions. A dense fog of anxiety enveloped me as I drew closer to home. Although I arrived in twenty minutes, it had felt like hours. I rushed into the house, Noel met me in the kitchen, and I fell into his arms. We hugged, surrounded by silent fear.

"What else did Dr. Pan say?" I whispered. "There must be something else."

"Nothing. Just that the blood test wasn't right and to come in first thing tomorrow."

"Are you sure? Think again. Didn't he at least mention something, anything?" my voice rose, as I tried to shake the conversation from Noel's memory.

"He said that I have elevated numbers in my liver and need further immediate testing," Noel said shakily.

I had no answer to that. I just wished that Dr. Pan had waited until morning to call. Waiting through the night would be a nightmare. I told Noel that it couldn't be too serious, as he was feeling great and looked healthy. After all, he had only seen the doctor for a routine checkup, with no ailments or complaints—how serious could it be? Besides, we were going to cruise the Panama Canal next month.

We decided to watch a movie, though for the life of me I cannot remember what we saw. The evening dragged on, each minute feeling like an hour. We tried to reassure each other, then slipped quietly into our own private despair. We slept fitfully, watching the clock as the seconds slid by. At last dawn broke and we got up weary from the night.

The next morning, Dr. Pan began, "I have some bad

news. Your blood tests came back showing unusual numbers. I think you might have cancer."

We sat stunned. I remember thinking how bad I felt for Dr. Pan to have to relay such devastating news.

"You must be wrong. I feel great!" Noel whispered.

"I'm afraid not," replied Dr. Pan. "I want to send you for a CAT scan immediately."

"What kind of cancer?" I asked shakily.

"I think pancreatic cancer, but the CAT scan will confirm the diagnosis."

"Isn't that what Randy Pausch, the author of *The Last Lecture*, has?" I asked, recalling his devastating YouTube video as he coped with his terminal disease.

But Dr. Pan was not familiar with Randy Pausch's story. He picked up the phone and scheduled the CAT scan at Hoag Hospital.

"But what is the prognosis for pancreatic cancer?" I persisted.

"Not very good," he almost whispered. "There is no cure, but there are a few treatments approved by the FDA." Dr. Pan excused himself and went to get some paperwork for us. Tears rolled down my cheeks as I held Noel's hand.

"This has to be wrong! You seem so well. It must be a mistake," I said adamantly, wanting to convince myself and console Noel.

Dr. Pan returned and handed Noel the CAT scan order. "I have spoken to one of my colleagues who is an oncologist. He can see you but would recommend that you get a second opinion at UCLA Medical Center, as they are involved in various experimental treatments."

"An oncologist? Oh, but I have one," I protested. "Dr. Vandermolen has been my oncologist since I had breast cancer in 2001. I know he would help Noel. But I still can't believe this diagnosis—Noel looks and feels great!"

"I hope I am wrong," Dr. Pan said. "I'll call you this afternoon after I get your CAT scan results. When we have more information, you'll be able to make an informed decision. Do you have any more questions?"

We did not. Dr. Pan shook Noel's hand and said how sorry he was.

Noel replied, "Thank you Doctor. I appreciate your time. I know how difficult this must be for a doctor to share bad news."

Our elevator ride down the six floors was silent. We drove directly to the Hoag facility in Huntington Beach. The CAT scan took less than an hour and then our wait began again. As we drove along Pacific Coast Highway toward Newport Beach, we pulled into a parking lot with a panoramic view of the ocean. The waves crashed and ran to shore; surfers bobbed over the waves, looking for a perfect ride; seagulls clustered around left-behind food in the parking lot, each maneuvering for his small morsel; wispy clouds dotted the sky; and the sun shone. Everything looked so normal, yet our world had been turned upside down by two words: pancreatic cancer.

As we walked into our house Bentley greeted us with his usual unwavering delight. I was struck again by the normalcy of our surroundings, though in my heart I knew our lives had dramatically shifted.

Dr. Pan called that afternoon. Noel had a mass in his

pancreas as well as growths in his liver and lymph nodes. "I'm going to schedule a liver biopsy to confirm it is cancer," he said. "We don't like to disturb the pancreas with a biopsy, but we can see if pancreatic cancer cells are in the liver. I suggest you call an oncologist immediately, as time is of the essence."

I began to cry. The night before, I had gone on-line to research pancreatic cancer. I knew what the diagnosis meant. As upset as I was, I realized Noel was terrified. I stopped crying and tried to reassure him. "Dr. Pan said we need to call an oncologist immediately."

"Can you make an appointment with Dr. Vandermolen?" Noel asked, his voice wavering.

Dr. Vandermolen's assistant, Julie, answered, and I explained our situation.

"Oh! I am so sorry for Noel," Julie said. "Dr. Vandermolen's associate, David Klein, is the pancreatic specialist. He's available on Monday, March seventeenth, at ten o'clock, at our other location on Old Newport Road,"

"Thanks, we will be there."

Seated next to Noel, both of us still in shock, I called Heather, Wendy, and Jeff with the diagnosis. They were all devastated. Wendy went into action. Her friend, Marisa. had surgery on a pancreatic tumor and was fine now. She would call Marisa and get back to us. In less than ten minutes Wendy had the name and number of Marisa's surgeon at UCLA, Dr. Ryber, and offered to call him for us.

Noel and I wandered around the house. We had one doctor's appointment, the name of a specialist, and a phone number for the Pancreatic Cancer Network in El

Segundo. In a terribly short time we had been flung into a new world of doctors, chemotherapy, differing opinions, and information about the pancreas. Now we quickly had to make decisions.

I jumped when the phone rang.

Wendy: "I called Dr. Ryber's office but since there are also tumors are outside the pancreas, he would not be able to do surgery. But I got the name and phone number of an oncologist who specializes in pancreatic cancer at UCLA. They say he's excellent—he thinks outside the box. Shall I make an appointment?"

Shocked to learn that Noel could not have surgery, I said, "Yes, please call—we need a second opinion."

In short order Wendy booked us an appointment for Thursday, March twentieth, at one o'clock. During the weekend, Noel grew quiet and withdrawn. He said he needed to think through all of the information. I tried to reassure him. I tried to be perky and fill up the hours with things to do, but the hours dragged by.

In Dr. Klein's office various people were sitting in comfortable chairs, reading magazines or sleeping, as they received their chemotherapy. Noel watched them until our turn came. The doctor came in quickly, armed with the CAT scan, blood test results, and Dr. Pan's findings. He did a quick exam of Noel, listened to his heart, took his blood pressure and pushed and prodded his stomach, looking for any discomfort. Noel did not have any pain or any symptoms, other than what the tests and scans had discovered. Dr. Klein sat down on the edge of the exam table. He recommended a chemotherapy regime of 5- FCU and

Cisplatin, every three weeks. These chemos were the only two approved by the FDA for pancreatic cancer treatment. He reiterated that because the cancer had spread, surgery was not an option. We asked if there was anything else we could do.

"No, that's our only option," he replied.

"What if I don't do anything?" Noël asked. "How quickly would the cancer spread?"

"If you don't do anything you may have two months. However with the chemo, we can hopefully shrink the tumors. Usually, by the time this cancer is found, it has spread, as in your case. I'm so sorry." Dr. Klein said, compassion in his eyes.

"We have an appointment at UCLA for a second opinion. Do you think he will have other options?" Noel asked hopefully.

"Unfortunately these are the only two chemos approved, but he may be able to try something different or experimentally. It's a good idea to seek a second opinion. Then you can let us know if you want to begin treatment here."

We thanked Dr. Klein and drove home silently. So much information had been given, but all I could hear were the words, "You may have two months." Two months? How was that possible? I looked at Noel, who seemed so healthy. His voice, nearly inaudible, snapped me back to reality. "Do you think we should still see the doctor at UCLA on Thursday?"

"Yes, definitely," I said with more voice than necessary. "I think we should at least talk to another doctor and see what he recommends. Then you would have more choices, hopefully. We have nothing to lose,"

As we pulled into the driveway, I noticed the roses in their first bloom of the year. Noel had painstakingly chosen each bush for its color and fragrance and planted them with care. Some of the blossoms swayed in the breeze, as if to welcome us home. Funny how everything around us was the same, while our world had turned upside down. It was St. Patrick's Day—and Heather's birthday, normally a fun-filled day. We had plans to celebrate with a family dinner at Maggiano's Little Italy, in South Coast Plaza. Noel did not want to change the plans; he would just take his afternoon nap before we left.

When we arrived at the restaurant, Heather, Derek, Declan, Wendy, Andy, Johnathan, and Austin, were waiting. We filled them in with the latest medical news and quickly changed the topic of conversation, trying to keep up a cheerful banter. Maggiano's is a great Italian restaurant, and we like to order family style after discussing what each of us wants to share. As usual, we ordered more than we could possibly eat, especially since most of us had lost our appetites. Dinner ended with a birthday dessert, and I was reminded of how we must cherish each and every moment. As we prepared to leave, each of the kids seemed to give Noel an extra long hug, as if to give him strength and show him how much he meant to them. We all seemed to have watery eyes.

It seemed like forever until Thursday. I spent hours on the Internet, researching everything I could find about Noel's disease. The more I read, the more I came to see that there was no cure; we were just trying to gain time. On the Pancreatic Cancer Network website, I located a live person who could answer my questions. The volunteers all have had some experience with this dreadful cancer. They are a great support group, especially for the caregivers. While I was soaking up each bit of information I could find, Noel informed me he did not want to read anything about it. He would follow the advice of whichever doctor we chose. I thought that was curious, as Noel always loved to research on the Internet, until I remembered my bout with breast cancer. I, too, had avoided reading about my disease. Maybe our willful ignorance is a defense mechanism: If we don't read about it, then it is not true. Or perhaps we do not want to know what lies in our future. Either way, it is the caregiver who tends to read up on the factual information and advice concerning the cancer, often withholding information, as well as the fear in their hearts, that they do not want to impose on their loved one.

Thursday morning dawned bright and cheery. We left Newport Beach early, as we worried about being late for our one o'clock appointment in Westwood with the oncologist I will refer to as Dr. UCLA. Of course, there was no traffic and we found his office with no problem. Since we were so early we went into the coffee shop and had a bit of lunch or, I should say, tried to eat a bit of lunch. Dr. UCLA's waiting room was a whole new world. A few people sat, one with a scarf to hide her bald head, another with a drip attached to a vein in his thin arm, and a couple of caregivers nervously flipped through magazines. A large framed picture of Albert Einstein was on one wall and I noticed a picture titled the "Dragon Slayer," by Brian Andreas. I had bought a copy of one of Andreas's pictures at Art for the Soul, on Balboa Island. Andreas is an artist, also called the Story People, who does fun colorful drawings accompanied by thought-provoking sayings. Another wall held pictures of various plants. All of a sudden, something moved from under a corner chair. I jumped and looked again. It was an adorable Shitzu, perfectly groomed and lounging as if he owned the place. Apparently he did. As one of the doors opened to the exam room the dog trotted through the waiting room and disappeared in the back of the office. *How strange*, I thought. *Whose dog is it, and why is it wandering the office?*

The staff worked behind a counter, with no window or partition separating them from the patients. A nurse handed us the necessary ever-growing paperwork, which we had to fill out for each doctor. As the designated scribe, I filled out page after page, then turned in the completed forms.

"The doctor will be with you in a minute. Oh, I need your insurance card so I can scan it into our system," she said.

As Noel handed over his Blue Cross insurance card, I sent up a quiet *thank you* that we had good coverage.

A man in toffee-colored pants and a button-down long-sleeve shirt came up to the counter, grabbed a file, and began reading it.

"Christopher," he said.

At first, Noel and I at first didn't move. Then we remembered that Noel's first name is Christopher, though he has always gone by his middle name, and followed the doctor into his inner sanctum. Dr. UCLA's office was filled with old framed prints of musical instruments, wall-to-wall bookshelves, and a desk cluttered with piles of papers and reports stacked like the Leaning Tower of Pisa. His windows looked out on the campus.

He got to the point. "Why are you here?"

I stammered, "You were recommended by Dr. Ryber's office. One of our friends had pancreatic surgery and since Noel cannot have surgery, Dr. Ryber's office suggested we get a second opinion. They said you were the best."

"They are right. Once you see me, you won't go anywhere else," he replied with arrogance in his voice. Dr. UCLA recounted his choice of treatment: four chemos. He would use 5 FCU and Cisplatin but would add two other chemos, non-FDA approved for pancreatic cancer. Noel would have the treatment for two days every three weeks. After the treatment, Noel would leave with the 5 FCU drip attached. I would have to learn to remove the needle and dress the area.

"What is the prognosis?" Noel asked.

"I am having some luck with shrinking the tumors."

"Will I get sick?"

"No, you'll feel great. Oh, you may have a bit of nausea but you should keep your stamina and also your hair."

"If we decide to do this, when will you begin?"

"Today is Thursday; we would begin on Monday. I would want you also to have a PortaCath implanted in your chest so we can give you these medicines without ruining your veins."

"We are planning a Panama Canal cruise next month. Can we start the treatment after the cruise?" I asked.

"If it were me, I would begin the treatment immediately, as there is always time for a cruise. Why don't you two go home and discuss this and give me a call."

"Thanks for your information. You've given me a ray of hope. We'll talk it over."

As Noel and I walked to the elevator, his step seemed a bit lighter, and he had a smile on his face.

"What do you think of Dr. UCLA and his treatment?" I asked.

"I'm excited, as he said there is hope. I wonder why all the other doctors are so grim about pancreatic cancer."

I didn't respond, knowing the usual outcome of the cancer and wanting to keep quality in our life. I was just happy that Noel's spirits had lifted.

"So, do you want to go to Dr. Klein or here?"

"I'd rather go closer to home, but I think we need to come here," Noel said matter of factly.

I leaned over and gave him a light kiss on the cheek, stroked his hand, and dialed the number for Dr. UCLA's office.

* * * * *

All through the months of chemotherapy and doctor's visits, I tried to keep my spirits up so Noel would not see my fear. By contrast, Noel had come to terms with the future a couple of days after his diagnosis Noel's love for the garden helped so much. He had inherited his green thumb from his father. In fall of 2007, when our future seemed to extend beyond the horizon, Noel had planted sweet pea seeds in our garden, just as his father used to do in Ireland. Noel had tended the seeds with care, babying them until they grew into prolific vines that climbed the strings he had woven to the side of the house. The sweet peas splashed an abundant palette of purple, red, white, pink, and lavender that never failed to lift our spirits. Noel liked to visit our local nurseries, Armstrong's and Roger's Gardens, particularly when the roses were in bloom. He always chose roses with fragrance, sniffing each one as we walked the paths of the nurseries before making his selection. The roses had flourished, too. And their fragrance drifted in the air whenever we walked near. Noel would often come in from the garden with a single rose for me, and say, "I met your boyfriend outside, and he asked me to give this to you."

I never tired of that game and the sweet sentiment behind the perfect single rose. And all through that anxious summer I was lucky to have bouquets of sweet peas and roses throughout the house, their fragrance filling our home. So abundant were the flowers that summer that we usually gathered bunches to share with Betty Dooley when we met for our Sunday chats.

One afternoon, after working in the garden, Noel was washing his hands at the kitchen sink when he said, "Annie, I was thinking about my ring."

I turned from the computer. "Your ring—which one?"

"My gold crested signet ring," he replied. "I was wondering who I should leave it to, since we have six grandsons."

His words stunned me, as I realized that he was thinking of what to do with his ring after he was gone. This ring had the Quinn family crest on it, along with an image of the head of an Irish wolfhound. Noel had said this was the Quinn's "symbol," but in researching it, I had never seen the wolfhound as part of the Quinn family's crest. I think Noel just chose to add it, as the wolfhound is the official dog of Ireland. Personally I loved that the dog's attributes are known to be loyalty, intelligence, and gentleness, plus a fierceness and protectiveness—so much like Noel. So maybe it was just his idea: the Christopher Noel Quinn crest.

With a lump in my throat, I quickly said, "Too bad you don't have six rings."

Noel was quiet for a moment, then said, "Maybe we could take the ring to William Harold Jewelers and ask whether they can make a mold and make five more rings."

I was surprised and then elated that Noel thought of our six grandsons in this way. The rings could be a legacy of his name and his love for each of them. How I hoped that it would be possible to make copies of the ring!

Endings

The Hooley

Noel wanted to visit our home in Ballycotton one last time. The chemotherapy seemed to be working, and the tumors were shrinking. Dr. UCLA said that as long as Noel felt well enough, we could travel between treatments. We told friends and family in Ireland we were coming home. Each one asked when they could see us, whether for dinner, tea, or just a chat, and our visit gathered momentum. I felt overwhelmed by the outpouring of love and the great number of people that cared about Noel. I also worried about the demands of such a visit on my husband.

One warm afternoon we were sitting in our garden, enjoying the fragrance of roses and sweet peas and the babble of the fountain, when Noel broke the silence. "Why don't we have an Irish Hooley?"

"A Hooley? What's that?" I said.

"You know, a Hooley, a party." Noel's eyes twinkled with hopeful enthusiasm.

It was a wonderful idea, although I was apprehensive about planning such an event in case Noel could not travel. But his excitement was infectious, and we spent the rest of the afternoon talking about how it might work. Over the next few weeks, our Hooley developed a life of its own. We decided to invite our family, including all six grandsons, and our three closest couple friends.

We wanted everyone to come, to bring their families and their children—everyone and anyone who had touched our lives. The guest list rapidly grew to a hundred and forty. I called the Bayview, our favorite hotel in Ballycotton, to inquire about dates. Miraculously, a wedding had just been cancelled for Saturday, September twentieth. We booked the dining room and reserved twenty rooms in the small hotel that overlooks Ballycotton Bay. The interior is rich with dark paneling, crimson leather furniture, patterned floral carpeting, and framed old pictures—just how one would envision a country estate. Their pub is warm and inviting. We called everyone we knew and told them to hold the date. Planning the Hooley was much like planning a small wedding. We worked on the menu for the five-course dinner, the flowers, the music, the invitation, and the travel plans—so many details that we would not leave to chance.

All the while, Noel continued his treatments and felt amazingly well. I knew that he was full of optimism, hope and happiness as we planned his trip home.

One afternoon we brought Noel's signet ring to William Harold Jewelers. This is a family-owned store, in business since 1969, on the corner across from Newport Beach City Hall on Balboa Peninsula. Noel and I had been doing business with them since 2000. Noel bought my diamond earrings there and had my engagement ring made there. I bought his gold watch there.

The owner of Harold Jewelers said the ring could be replicated. The new rings would be ready in a couple of weeks.

"That's great," Noel said. I can give the boys their rings in Ireland, when we have the Hooley."

I did the math. If Noel gave the six grandsons their rings in September, he would not have his to wear, which he loved to do. I suggested that he order six duplicates, so that he could continue to wear the original.

* * * * *

When we arrived at our home in Ballycotton, we set up housekeeping for all our kids and grandsons. A few days before the Hooley, when we were all together, Noel asked the family to come to the living room. He began to talk about the significance of the Irish wolfhound in the country's mythology and the Quinn signet ring. Then Noel produced six black William Harold Jewelers bags, each containing a small box lined in blue velvet. He called each boy up individually, from Scott, the oldest, to Austin, the youngest, opened the box, showed each boy the ring, and placed it on their little finger for a moment. He told them that when they grew older they could wear the ring as a remembrance from Granda Quinn. He replaced each ring in its box and gave it to the boys with an extra special Granda hug. As the moms and dads took custody of the rings, there were no dry eyes in the room.

* * * * *

September 21, 2008. Four a.m. on Sunday morning. I was curled up in an overstuffed chair, tucked warmly in a blanket, looking out the window. The parking lot was filled with cars quietly waiting for the dawn. The lighthouse stood sentinel over the sleepy harbor, bathed in the light of a full moon. Noel, my love, snored peacefully in our suite. Too excited to sleep, I kept reliving the evening, the Hooley swirling in my head to the tempo of an Irish jig. A night to remember, a night that I never wanted to end.

It seemed only moments ago that we had dressed to go downstairs to the party. Noel looked dapper and distinguished in his navy blue sport coat, gray slacks, and a light blue shirt unbuttoned at the collar with no tie. (He had stipulated a tie-less event.) He was tanned from the Southern California sun and his gray hair, just a bit thin from the chemo, was perfectly combed. His eyes twinkled in expectation, but I had butterflies in my stomach as we walked hand in hand down the corridor toward our Hooley. As we entered the lobby the traditional Irish band played a jig as family and friends crowded in for hugs and photos and conversation. Drinks and hors d'oeuvres were passed around while the grandsons ran around with their Irish cousins, making the evening joyful and merry. Noel looked around the room and beamed with joy.

Dinner was served at seven. Place cards guided the guests to their tables—as was my habit, I had mixed young and old, Irish and American, friends and family. Twinkling votive candles bordered the table arrangements of bright yellow, orange, and pink Gerbera daisies. Light green laminated bookmarks, with "Enjoy the Moments" emblazoned on the front and "Noel and Annie Quinn, Irish-American Hooley, September 20, 2008" stamped on the back, were placed by each guest's plate. Everyone cheered when Noel stood to welcome all to the Hooley, from California to Amsterdam, North Carolina to Shannon, Nashville to London, and County Cork. He toasted our friends and family and thanked them for their support and love. Then he asked Betty, his sister-in-law, to say the blessing. Dinner was marvelous! Irish cream of potato soup or salad, followed by a main course choice of steak, chicken, or fresh fish. The children were served a special meal. During the meal, a cacophony of conversation and laughter filled the room. For dessert, guests chose from among apple cobbler, profiteroles, homemade ice cream, and the cheese board. Noel also surprised me with an anniversary cake. Ten years ago, on the twenty-second of September, we had met in Connemara.

After dinner, Noel took the microphone. He spoke of the love he had for each person in the room. He was still overwhelmed by the outpouring of love, compassion, and care everyone had shown him. He reflected on the past ten years, from our destined meeting on this beloved coast to the blending of Irish and American cousins, family, and friends. The love in the room was palpable. Noel sat down and we held hands under the table. The microphone was passed to other friends and family who told a story and spoke of the love they felt for Noel and the wonder of this evening amid the laughter, tears, jeering, and applause.

Later, our guests gravitated to other parts of the hotel. Some sat in the small foyer, others went in to the pub, and the children ran in circles around the large round table and up and down the stairs. No one wanted the evening to end. A few people began to sing their party pieces, the tradition I fell in love with when I first visited Noel's family in Ireland. The songs were as diverse as the group. Jerry, Noel's brother-in-law, sang, "I am the Music Man," accompanied by all the hand gestures. Many of the adults and children joined in. Noel's teenage nieces sang "Somewhere Over the Rainbow," Noel's brother Mick sang Frank Sinatra songs, and Mick's wife, Therese, offered her elegant recital of the poem, "If I was A Lady." Not to be outdone, our American sons-in-law sang, "Take Me Out to the Ball Game," and my six little grandsons belted out Johnny Cash's "[Burning] Ring of Fire." Then everyone sang John Denver's "Annie's Song" to me. The Hooley's spontaneous outpouring of talent and love continued into the wee hours.

Noel was tiring. We said our good nights, gave hugs and kisses, and walked slowly to the elevator. Upstairs we sauntered happily down the corridor to our room. When Noel opened the door, moonlight shone through the window. A contented feeling enveloped us as we silently hugged. A tear rolled down my face. The Irish-American Hooley was over, but it was etched forever in our hearts and minds as the symbol that celebrated our life and love.

Our friends and family departed for their homes in various parts of the world, leaving us to spend a few days at our home in Ballycotton before we dove back into the world of chemotherapy, doctors, and tests. One day, I encouraged Noel to fish from the concrete jetty in the harbor, which he had not done since he was a boy. It was fun watching him cast the line way out into the sea, reel it slowly in, never showing disappointment at the lack of a fish on the line, and then slinging the line ever father into the sea in gleeful anticipation. One afternoon, we took a leisurely drive, as we had so many times before, and noticed a lane we had never explored. It led to the opposite shore of Ballycotton Bay, where we discovered a perfect whitewashed bungalow with a thatched roof and a garden that extended to the sea. The sun was setting and the clouds themselves reflected autumn's colors of orange, red and yellow. Birds swooped down to skim the water's edge. We stood without uttering a word as we joined hands, captivated by the magic of nature, the warmth of our love, and the serenity of the moment.

Saying Good-bye

utumn of 2008 was bittersweet. Noel was following the presidential campaign with great interest. He very much admired the Democratic candidate. When friends asked what they could do to help, he had a ready reply: "Vote for Obama."

But our Republican friends, who would have done most anything for Noel, would reply, "Oh, anything but that."

An important part of Noel's journey through pancreatic cancer involved our *Noel's Fan Club* electronic newsletter, which I circulated from California to Ireland and from Australia to North Carolina. I reported, sometimes daily, on Noel's diagnosis, his treatments, his response, his medicines, and our responses as we traversed this crazy world of pancreatic cancer. The fan club responded with prayers, thoughts, and support. I often printed the emails so he could see all the love and support from around the world. Noel was receiving back all he had given to his family and friends over the years, and he was humbled and amazed by it. I was simply grateful, as it made his journey much easier.

In November, Chrystal visited and introduced us to her boyfriend, Ben. I think she wanted Noel's approval. He and Ben hit it off instantly, and even though Chrystal was young, Noel felt it was a good match. As the holidays came, although no one said it, we all wanted to be together for what looked to be our last Christmas and New Year's with Noel. Jeff and his family planned to visit for ten days, staying nearby at Newport Dunes on the bay. Before picking them up at the airport, Noel and I went to their place and decorated with Christmas lights and a small tree.

With six little grandsons from almost two to age six, Christmas was a bit crazy, but fun. Christmas dinner was Noel's favorite meal. We did it all: turkey, ham, and prime rib, plus mashed potatoes, vegetables, pie and English trifle. After dinner, we sat, stuffed, the boys tired from all the excitement of the day. Noel looked content amidst of the glow of what he called our "true family Christmas," as we surveyed the festive decor of snowmen, angels, candles, and Santa Claus, trying to make these moments last.

After Christmas Noel went for another round of chemotherapy. Dr. UCLA told us that Noel's markers were gradually going up. The good news was that the tumor in the pancreas was stable, but the tumors in the liver had doubled. The doctor wanted a new chemo regimen at his office, followed by pills for fourteen days. Noel was thrilled by what he thought was good news. Although the elephant in the room was not discussed, I knew that the chemotherapy was being changed because the cancer cells had grown immune to the current medicine. We grasped at the hope of more time.

New Year's Eve was happy and chaotic. The boys played while we talked, laughed, shared memories, ate, and counted down to midnight. We snapped a photo for our annual St. Patrick's Day card. Noel tired and excused himself before the ball dropped in Times Square. I watched, slipping into melancholy, as each of the boys gave their Granda a hug and a kiss. He hugged each of the boys a little longer, looked into their eyes with all his wisdom, and wished them a "good night and happy 2009."

After Jeff and his family flew home, filled with memories and a lifetime of hugs, January was a difficult time. Noel was not responding well to the new treatment. He felt lethargic and spacey. I took the little brass bell we had bought on a whim in Albuquerque and set it on his bedside table, in case he needed my help. But Noel rarely used it. I called Dr. UCLA more often, asking about various medicines for the nausea and other symptoms of the chemo. Meanwhile, Noel had begun another round of treatment when he was not yet stable from the last. I wondered whether all of this was working, but the doctor would only answer Noel's questions, and Noel had none. I, on the other hand, had gone on the Web to learn more about the side effects of this chemo, where I discovered that patients with severe breathing problems should avoid this medicine. Besides having pancreatic cancer, Noel had been diagnosed in 2006 with COPD. (Chronic obstructive pulmonary disease, a disease that interferes with normal breathing and worsens over time.) Now he was having more difficulty breathing, even with his inhalers. I asked the doctor about this, too, but he insisted that this was the treatment he recommended. I felt helpless, as Noel did not want to question any of the treatments nor would he read anything, I mean, anything at all, on his prognosis. I did not want to take away his hope for remission, but the treatment was definitely affecting his quality of life. Over the past ten years, Noel and I had always discussed everything. Now, my best friend and confidant was the one person I could not share with.

On January eleventh Noel was not well enough to go to Mass. I knew he must feel terrible, as he seldom missed a Sunday. I kept asking the doctor to change various nausea medicines and whether we should change any of the treatments. Noel developed severe constipation despite being on laxatives. It was so bad at one point that he asked me to take him to the hospital for relief. Luckily the extra medications worked and we avoided having to visit the hospital. But the treatments continued throughout the month.

On February fifth, as we sat in Dr. UCLA's waiting room, I was struck by all of the other caregivers surrounding me. The patients here usually sat in resigned indifference as the caregivers frantically monitored their appointments, checked blood work, verified insurance, and sought proper medication, always searching for the elusive cure to give one more second, minute, hour, or year of life. Caregiving is an elusive word for the person in charge of managing another's life. Despite my feelings of helplessness, I had become fairly expert on the side effects of chemotherapies, medicines to combat nausea, diarrhea, constipation, throat constriction, and extreme fatigue. We caregivers try to stay one step ahead of the treatment, though in truth we are usually two steps behind. We have no control but try desperately to give our loved ones comfort, peace, and time. We often feel like deer caught in the headlights as fear envelops us along with the understanding that we cannot change the future, but must keep up an outward appearance of complete control and serenity. When Noel's appointment was called, he was told he faced another round of chemotherapy. He decided to continue with treatment even though the markers had not changed.

February twenty-first was a terrible day. Noel's breathing grew more labored and he developed pneumonia, caused, I was convinced, by the latest chemotherapy. I turned to Dr. Morrica, his pulmonologist. After giving him a shot and medicine, Dr. Morrica recommended that we get oxygen at the house to help him breathe. I asked about the chemotherapy, and he said it might be causing some of the difficulty but did not really know. The only good news was that Noel's stomach felt better.

February twenty-eighth turned sad. Noel felt worse and slept most of the day. When he got up, we had some homemade chicken soup, and, as he sat in his recliner, we talked. I broached the topic of his next round of chemotherapy and asked how he felt about continuing. We talked for a long while, and he finally decided that he felt too sick to go the next round.

I was surprised when Noel added that he feared death. But as we talked he explained that he feared the unknown of the continued symptoms and the eventual, final pain. I promised that I would make sure he would have no pain. Finally, we were facing the elephant in the room, and all my worries, concerns, and expertise spilled out. I told him about hospice and shared my knowledge of the process, the main one being the use of morphine to alleviate any pain. I again promised he would not be in pain, secretly praying that I could keep my pledge. We talked late into the evening, remembering our good times together.

"Do you regret we didn't get to Paris and the Panama Canal?" I said.

He looked at me, and said, "You know, Annie, my only regret in dying is leaving you."

And then I cried—tears of sadness, sure, but also relief that finally we had discussed the inevitable. I could talk to my best friend again about everything. Together we would see what Dr. UCLA had to say on Thursday.

We did see the doctor, who said Noel's markers were up a bit. He wanted to change the course of treatment again. Noel questioned him about that, and I asked the doctor what he would do if it were he, continue or stop all treatment.

"You know what I would do. I would take the medicine," he said quickly. "But why don't you go home and talk about it. Call me if you want to continue with my treatment and expertise."

And with that he escorted us to the door of his office. We left a bit shell shocked. In the parking garage, we found the car and sat for a bit. All the hope given to us over the last eight months was gone. Now Noel had another decision to make.

The decision loomed as Noel continued to feel unwell. I guess Noel was waiting to see the results of the latest blood work. On March ninth, we saw Dr. Moricca for Noel's pneumonia re-check. He had put him on oxygen 24/7 and Prednisone. I also had weaned him off most of his nausea medicine. (I was lucky enough to speak to a friend of Mike Brenna's, a pharmacist at the City of Hope, who explained to me all the medicines Noel was on and their side effects. He said the dosages were too high and suggested I cut them back.) Oddly, each time I had called Dr. UCLA about Noel's extreme nausea, the doctor had added another medicine but never told me to stop the others.

Noel began to feel better. He was more wakeful and felt less nauseated. Also he had not had any chemo since February twelfth. We spoke with Dr. Moricca about the chemo and Noel's decision. I also had seen Dr. Vandermolen, for my quarterly breast cancer checkup and discussed Noel's situation. Dr. Vandermolen was sympathetic and compassionate. He would accept Noel as a patient if he decided to stop treatment at UCLA. We also discussed hospice.

Noel decided to stop treatment. We called Dr. UCLA's office and told them the news. We never heard from him again. Noel was dropped, like a hot potato. Luckily, Dr. Vandermolen was in the wings to support and guide us through the remainder of this difficult journey. He examined Noel, answered his questions, and joked and laughed with him just as they had done when I was in treatment in 2002. He urged us to call in hospice whenever we felt it was the right time.

As March unfolded, Noel felt better day-by-day. We celebrated Heather and Wendy's birthdays. Noel even asked if I was making Heather's cake, an angel food cake with whipped cream and fresh strawberries, which he loved. And then, on March twenty-ninth, Noel began to cough again. He would panic when he could not catch his breath. He asked me to call in hospice.

On April second, John and Destiny (how ironic for the nurse to have that name) arrived from hospice to examine

Noel, fill out the paperwork, and order all the medications and oxygen. They were a godsend, efficient, compassionate, upbeat, funny, and very informative. They were also surprised to find that Noel was not in pain, considering the severity of pancreatic cancer. They explained that most people did not call in hospice when they first decide not to continue treatment, even though it simplifies life, with no trips to the doctor or pharmacy. Every six months Noel's case would be re-evaluated. They also told us about one of their patients who had been on hospice for five years. Noel really liked them and felt a bit of relief when they explained their procedures. Before day's end we had a new oxygen tank, paperwork completed, and medicines. Hospice turned to be a wonderful organization, filled with compassionate people.

By the middle of April, Noel was suffering from jaundice, ascites stomach (bloating), tiredness, and a bit of confusion. Twice a week the hospice nurses showed up to take his blood pressure, check his oxygen levels, and talk with him. They treated Noel like a person, not a number, and all of them loved his Irish accent and quick wit. In the midst of all this medical madness, Noel retained the twinkle in his eye and his ability to enjoy some mighty *craic*. I was often reminded of the card I bought, when I had breast cancer:

What Cancer Cannot Do
Cancer is so limited
It cannot cripple Love,
It cannot shatter Hope,
It cannot corrode Faith

It cannot destroy Peace
It cannot kill Friendship
It cannot suppress Memory
It cannot silence Courage
It cannot invade the Soul
It cannot steal Eternal Life
It cannot conquer the Spirit
—Anonymous

On April sixteenth I wrote in my journal that I was watching Noel slip slowly away. "What am I going to do when I can't talk to Noel anymore? No phone calls...no letters...no anything? How am I going to cope?" And then I wrote. "Don't cry because it is over, Smile because it happened," a favorite Dr. Seuss quote I often used, which I truly believed. Because however lost I, let alone my kids and grandsons, would be without the gift of Noel's wisdom, strength, and compassion, he had taught us all how to live. Now he was teaching us how to die.

April 19. Chrystal called today, so excited. She wanted us to know that she and Ben were engaged to be married in the summer of 2010. Then she asked for Noel.

"I want you to give me away and walk me down the aisle," she said.

At first, Noel could not speak. Then with tears in his eyes, he said, "I only would love to. I really like Ben. But I don't think I will be able to. You are so special and I know your wedding will be wonderful."

When I took the phone back, all I heard on the other end were sobs. "I really want Noel to give me away."

"I know," I said. "And I know he would if he could, but I don't think he will last until next summer. But he loves you."

April 22. Wendy wanted to have Austin's second birthday at our house, as Noel was not well enough to go out. When Austin needed help with opening one of his presents, he turned to his Granda. Noel, hooked up to oxygen, took out his trusty Swiss Army knife, cut away the plastic shrink-wrap packaging, and handed the toy to Austin—a sweet moment in time. The party continued with cake, ice cream, and lots of laughter. Noel was tired and bid his good night. Again everyone lined up for Noel's special hug and then he was off.

April 23. Hospice arrived this morning and took Noel's vitals. He was chipper and funny. The hospice nurse was in love with Noel's Irish brogue and sense of humor. She chatted and laughed while she worked, promising to return the following Monday. While he was taking his afternoon nap I thought I would run to the post office. When I returned, Noel was sitting on the side of the bed. Suddenly he doubled over in pain. He held his back and stomach and cried out. I called hospice, my hands shaking as I dialed the number. All I could think of was my promise—no pain.

"Noel is in terrible pain. What do I do?"

"Get the medication, oxycodene or morphine, give him 5ml., then jump to 10ml. between three-thirty and four-thirty p.m. We will send someone out later to check on him," said the efficient voice on the other end of the line.

I gave Noel the first dose, got him settled back in bed, and called the girls in a panic. First Heather. No answer, so I left a rambling message. "Come down. Noel's in terrible pain. Come quick. Call me back." Then I called Wendy. "Call Heather, and come right away. Noel is in terrible pain. I'm scared!"

Noel was a bit more restful with all the medication. Then I called Jeff.

"Jeff," my voice in full panic. "Talk to me, talk to me. Calm me down. Noel is really bad. I can't fall apart now. Talk to me. I can't fall apart. Not now." I rambled on.

Jeff handed the phone to Scott, who said, "Hi, Grandma."

I was shocked back to reality.

"Hi, Scott. How are you? What are you doing?" I tried to sound normal.

Scott continued to talk, though I have no recollection of what was said. Jeff came back on the line and I explained what had happened. After we hung up, I wandered back into the bedroom.

By the time Heather and Wendy appeared around six o'clock, Noel was comfortable enough to joke with them. They saw the terror in my eyes and the incomprehension in Noel's eyes. They asked Noel what he wanted for dinner and he requested fruit. I continued to give him morphine as directed by hospice. The hospice nurse arrived and took Noel's vitals. My call had surprised them, as they thought Noel had at least another month. The hospice nurse left, promising to return if needed, and we were left on our own. Noel was resting comfortably, so late in the evening I told the girls to get some rest and come back in the morning. It had been such a relief to have the girls with me and to understand my depth of love for Noel. Now they reluctantly agreed to go.

All through the night, Noel and I continued our chats, and then, just before he fell into deep sleep, he said, "Annie, life is about a laugh and a joke," and he laughed.

"Why are you laughing?" I asked, clutching his hand.

"I can't remember the joke," he said, squeezing my hand before he drifted off.

Those were Noel's last words. He still breathed as I lay next to him, reflecting on our few years together. He had been laughing over a book when I first noticed him, and now, even at the end, he was still laughing. I don't think I had ever felt so alone. I kept saying, "I love you, forever and ever and ever." Childlike, I kept repeating, "You promised you would never leave me." How selfish I sounded! Around four o'clock in the morning, noon Irish time, I called Noel's brother, Mick. They were to arrive on the following Tuesday for a short visit. I told him Noel was resting peacefully and in no pain. He decided not to change his flight. This, I was sure, would please Noel, as he did not want people flying in to say good-bye and sit and stare at him. He, who normally loved visitors, wanted quiet, his normal routine, and to not exert himself with chat. In short, no fuss.

By the time the girls returned early the next morning, Noel had slipped into a coma. Joan arrived shortly before noon. When she saw that the girls needed to be with me, she offered to pick up Jeff at LAX. I lay next to Noel, unable to believe he was in the final stage of his physical departure. The day dragged. Jeff appeared at the bedroom door at 2:40 in the afternoon and surveyed the scene. I got up and hugged him, crying softly into his shoulder. Joan said good-bye and said to call if we needed anything. And then all my kids and I gathered around the bed. Noel's breath softly rattled. He took a few more short breaths with long pauses between. I kept saying, really to no one, "Has he stopped breathing? No, are you sure?" Then stillness enveloped me as Noel, as quietly as he had lived, left us on April twenty-fourth at 3:05 p.m.

And I began to cry.

A Simple Mass

Though we need to weep your loss,
You dwell in that safe place in our hearts,
Where no storm or night or pain can reach you.

Your love was like the dawn
Brightening over our lives,
Awakening beneath the dark
A further adventure of colour,…

—On the Death of the Beloved
John O'Donohue

Noel wanted a simple Mass, with his ashes scattered in the places that meant so much to him. His idea of a simple Mass involved a short homily, an even shorter eulogy, and, most important, the Eucharist. As a Roman Catholic, Noel believed that the Eucharist—the sacrament of bread and wine that Christians of all varieties partake of during communion—is in reality, not merely symbolically, converted into Christ's body and blood. Noel accepted his church's doctrine that this conversion is so complete that Christ's body and blood, soul and divinity, is truly, really, and substantially contained in the sacrament of the Eucharist, with only the *appearance* of bread and wine remaining. Although we had many lengthy discussions on this topic, I never quite understood how the bread and wine truly became Christ's body and blood or why it was such an important issue. Noel never tried to persuade me, but he held fast to his core belief.

Heather and Wendy accompanied me to a meeting at Our Lady of Mount Carmel Church on Balboa Peninsula to plan the details. Even though we were not Catholic, we wanted to respect the church's traditions and to honor Noel's requests. We also wanted to embrace everything important to friends and family of several denominations that were to attend. Because the ashes or body were not present, a memorial Mass was in order. The eulogy would be limited to three minutes. (Noel would appreciate that.) We were given a booklet from which we could choose appropriate scripture readings. We spoke about the music and received a list of available singers. We booked the service for Thursday morning, April twenty-ninth. All three of the Irish priests that Noel had known, however, were unavailable, and given my upcoming journey to Ireland for a memorial Mass with Noel's family, I could not wait. The church's Vietnamese priest, Father Robert Tan Pham S.J., had a sincere passion for the church. He was difficult to understand but available. We later telephoned the musician, Ann Peter, the wonderful singer I so enjoyed. Ann suggested various ideas, and I was thrilled when she promised to include some Irish ballads.

My children and friends who knew and loved Noel wrote the eulogy. Gary Kilgore read it eloquently, often with a tear in his eye. "I've never met anyone like Noel," he said. "He never judged nor did he condemn anyone's actions; he just merely accepted them as they were. He was a unifier and constantly would bring those he loved together for a great time and a shared laugh. His smile would warm your heart."

Yes, his smile did that, from the night we met.During the Mass, Father Tan Pham kept referring to Noel as "No El." Johnathan, age five, finally leaned over to me and asked, "Who was 'No El?'"

I must say something about the two acolytes that assisted Father Tan Pham at the Mass. During our travels around the United States, Noel and I had seen few African Americans in the Roman Catholic churches we visited— and never at Mount Carmel. Noel found this curious, for in Ireland he had known African Roman Catholics. After her death, Mary's wedding ring had been sent to Nigeria, where the church had an outreach. But African-Americans here, I tried to explain, were traditionally brought up in various Protestant churches, and I assumed that having not been raised Catholic, they were unlikely to convert, unless through marriage or a missionary experience. So I was surprised to see two African American acolytes enter the pulpit to serve at Noel's Mass. Noel would have loved it. During the next two weeks my curiosity got the better of me. I called the church and learned that the family was from Africa and had joined the church in 2008. They attended a different Sunday service than Noel and I had.

On Mother's Day I rented a Duffy electric boat to honor Noel's wish that some of his ashes be spread in Newport Harbor. We had on board six sunflowers, one for each of our grandsons. Heather, Derek, Declan, Wendy, Andy,

Johnathan, Austin, Gary, Yvette, and I motored to the entrance of the harbor, and, as Gary steered the boat in circles, Heather and Wendy cast the ashes over the side. Then our grandsons and I tossed the six sunflowers onto the water. The sunflowers floated in a circular motion, surrounding the ashes until they slowly began to sink.

I planned a simple Mass in June at Ballycotton's Star of the Sea Catholic Church with a reception to follow at the Bayview Hotel. I notified Noel's family and friends in Ireland, as well as my family and friends in America, of the date. A simple Mass and another celebration of Noel's life would allow all his Irish friends and family to pay their respects.

One Thursday morning in May, however, my plans suddenly changed. I was on the phone with Denise McGrath, in Ballycotton, when she mentioned she was attending Noel's Mass that afternoon in Cork City.

"What?" I said. "What Mass are you talking about? Lilian is having a family Mass today for her immediate family, but how did you hear about it?"

"Oh, a Mass memorial for Noel Quinn was in the Irish Examiner this morning. I am going to go," said Denise.

I was stunned. In Ireland, people still read the obituaries and "Mass notices", and try to attend the funeral and offer their condolences to the family. I was keenly aware of this tradition because Noel read the Irish Examiner's obituary and Mass notices late at night on the computer in California. He would often call his family to notify them of a death and call the family of the deceased to offer his sympathy. I knew this was important to Noel and his Irish heritage.

I also knew that many in County Cork would read this Mass announcement and attend. Since Noel was born in Cork City and had so many friends and family in the area, I knew the Mass would be well attended. I immediately called off the Mass planned for June, as we could not have a Mass a month. Noel would not approve, as he only wanted a Simple Mass.

In October I returned to Ballycotton with Noel's ashes. I planned to scatter some on Mary's grave, give some to Noel's brother, Mick, for the Quinn family plot, and float some on Ballycotton Bay. Noel had told me that Sean McGrath would help me place the ashes on his sister Mary's grave, and I asked Sean whether the local priest could first bless the ashes. I assumed that the priest would say a few words in a simple ceremony. Of course my assumption was wrong; Roman Catholic priests will follow someone's ashes anywhere. Sean informed me that the priest would be happy to say Mass for Noel on Thursday morning at Star of the Sea Church and bless the ashes. Oh no! I had packed Noel's ashes in Baggies, not a formal urn—how do you put a Baggie of ashes on the altar? I was also concerned about holding a third Mass. All Noel had wanted was a simple Mass, and I wanted to honor that. So I did not invite anyone else to the Mass on Thursday other than Sean, Denise, and Betty.

I had separated the ashes into three Baggies. Now I had to find a special container for the Mass. Heather and I visited the studio of a well-known local potter, Stephen Pearce, situated across Ballycotton Bay from our home. In his gallery I found a fine yellow ceramic sugar bowl that would suit the occasion, a simple urn with a lid.

"Sister Eilesh, or Betty, as many of us know her, wanted to know if she could do some special readings at the graveside if the priest was not going to the graveside.

"Oh, I am sure the priest is not coming to the gravesite." I said in a very confident voice. "If you want to read something, that is fine."

As Heather, Derek, Declan, and I got ready to leave the house, I gathered a few lilies, stock, and chrysanthemums from the various bouquets friends had brought over and made a simple arrangement to lay on the grave.

Star of the Sea Church, built of stone in 1901, is beautifully situated on a hill overlooking the bay. Holding the yellow sugar bowl with my beloved inside, I approached Father Aiden, he took the sugar bowl, and placed it on the altar. Word of the Mass had spread throughout the village, and neighbors as well as several family members from Ballycotton, Ballyrobin, Ballyadreen, and County Cork attended. Father Aiden had known Noel, and his simple homily reflected eloquently on Noel's life. After the Mass ended, I walked outside, moved again by the beauty of this small village by the bay, when a woman approached.

"Oh my goodness," she said, as she grabbed my hand. "When I spoke to your sister I didn't realize that is who died!"

Flabbergasted, I replied, "You spoke to my sister?"

"Yes, and I had no idea that is who died. I worked in the bank in Douglas, and I would often see Noel. I can't believe that is who your sister was talking about."

"My sister? But she lives in California. Where did you meet her?"

"Oh, I met her a couple of days ago in Ballycotton. She was in front of your house."

"Oh, you mean my sister-in-law, Therese?"

"Yes, I saw her on a walk in Ballycotton, and she said that her brother-in-law had died and owned a house in Ballycotton. I am so sad it was Noel, as he was such a lovely man. He was so excited when he went to California. I heard he was happy. I had no idea that he had died. I am so sorry for your loss."

"Thank you," I said, as we parted.

We all moved toward to the parking area. Once inside the car, I removed two of the Baggies from the sugar bowl urn and placed them under the seat. I noticed that the priest was climbing into a car that was also headed for the graveyard where Mary was buried. I looked around for Sean but did not see him. Heather drove us to the nearby village of Cloyne, and the graveyard at St. Coleman Parish Catholic Church. I got out of the car, holding tight to the yellow sugar bowl and the flowers I had gathered together in my kitchen. Sheila, Noel's sister-in-law, also carried a small bouquet, and Betty carried a special book.

I had never visited Mary's gravesite. Sean had told me that crushed white rock covered the grave, and I had suggested that we keep it simple and just sprinkle some ashes over the rocks. But as we approached the actual gravesite I noticed a hole in the middle of the gravesite. I looked at Sean for explanation.

"I got a sledgehammer," he said.

"A sledgehammer?"

"Yes, I didn't know that under the white rock the grave

was covered in concrete. So I went into the church and found a sledgehammer and made a hole."

Thoughts of us being arrested as grave robbers swirled in my head. I looked at Sean and back at the hole.

"I thought you wanted to put the urn in the grave," Sean said, as he took the urn from my hands. He tried to place the urn in the hole, but the hole still wasn't wide enough. Sean handed me the urn, ready to have another go with the sledgehammer.

I thought quickly. "Wait, we can put the Baggie inside the hole," I said, as I opened the lid, pulled out the Baggie, and handed it to Sean.

Sean placed the Baggie of ashes into the hole, Father Aiden prayed, and Betty read the beautiful elegy by the Irish poet, John O'Donohue, "On the Death of the Beloved." Years later she would recall how lonely and lost Noel had been after Mary's death. Her first inkling that Noel might have found someone special was when his nightly phone calls stopped. Then, said Betty, "I realized that he had bought a computer! And then he was going to California for Christmas! It was wonderful to meet them on their visits to Ireland and see how happy they both were—I now know that I have gained a sister. Isn't it amazing that we have to lose to find—if Mary had not died, I would not have met Annie. My life would have been much poorer for that...."

I treasure those words.Sheila and I placed our bouquets on the grave. All the while I gazed at the hole in the middle of the grave, and thought, *Noel just wanted a simple Mass.*

When it was over, Sean said he would get some cement and fill the hole. We decided to put Noel's name on the headstone: Christopher Noel Quinn—December 13, 1939 to April 24, 2009—Cork/California. Betty said she would plant a holly bush, Noel's favorite, and a fuchsia to add color to the grave. After a short time we drifted back to our cars. I retrieved the remaining Baggies from under the seat and put them into the sugar bowl.

Sean and Denise had invited us to their home above McGrath's Pub. Betty had baked current scones and brought some homemade jam. We enjoyed them along with ham and cheese sandwiches and tea, as we remembered Noel and the lovely way we had met. Now, here I was with his first wife's brother and sister, and I felt all over again his presence and his love.

Two days later, Mick and Therese came to Ballycotton. It turned out that they wanted a part of Noel in the family plot. Mick whispered to me, "Do you have something for me?"

I understood his question. I reorganized the remaining Baggie of ashes destined for Ballycotton Bay, placed some in the yellow sugar bowl, and handed it over to Mick. Later he would place it in the Quinn family gravesite in Cork.

The simple Mass Noel had requested had grown into three very different ceremonies, each fraught with emotion and complicated family dynamics. Yet how could it have been any different, despite our best intentions to keep it simple? Noel's legacy embraces Mary's McGrath family, the Quinns, and my own family in California. Through the magic of our meeting and falling in love, we all came together—simple and complex, all mixed up together.

Shell Struck in Ballycotton

I wanted to say a private farewell to Noel by the ocean, such an important part of our lives. One afternoon I walked down the narrow village road carrying the last physical remains of my love in a Baggie. I was almost to Ballycotton Harbor when I spotted the half-hidden staircase that descends to the rocky beach. Noel and I had spent many hours there, walking hand in hand along the sand, marveling at the tide's ebb and flow, breathing in the water's life force. Here was where we came to seek serenity, to find peace. This was the perfect place, near the lighthouse. I cautiously stepped onto the wooden stairs, half covered by thorny blackberry bushes, weeds, crushed shells and wet sand. At the bottom, I walked unevenly over rocks, seaweed, and sand to the ocean. Tears streamed down my cheeks as I cast the ashes into the water and watched the tide slowly take them into the waters. This time the beach brought no solace.

I do not think I have ever walked a beach without coming upon another addition to my collection of shells and sea glass. Throughout my life, shell collecting had always been a connection to my past. Now, during my lonely farewell to Noel, I had no desire to search out the perfect shell. Without Noel I had no future, and the recent past was too painful to recall.

I pulled my windbreaker close to me and I turned to leave. Unthinking, I glanced down at the sand. A large fan shell lay just before me. The perfectly shaped shell was a muted peachy brown with a hint of pinkish orange on the top and an opaque alabaster bottom, with a small thumbprint fan shape. The shell had perfect ridges and symmetry—no chips, no rough edges—an unexpected gift from the sea. Cradling this survivor in my hand I continued along the rocky beach, and out of habit scanned the sand as I headed toward the stairs. And there, amidst all the crushed rocks and smashed shells I spied a second fan shell, smaller but the perfect companion for the one in my hand. I picked it up and compared the two. I looked around, but saw no other fan shells. I had never seen this type of shell on the beaches of

These two shells will always hold a special place in my heart.

Ballycotton nor on any other beach I had combed around the world. Later I learned that these shells are known as Pecten Albican Flat Sea Scallop, common to the seas off Japan and China, where they are usually found at a depth of 80 meters. These shells symbolize the Greek goddess Aphrodite and the Roman goddess Venus, who symbolize love. The two shells lifted my spirits and renewed my belief in eternal love, as if the ocean itself were telling me that its intangible, constant gifts would always surround me. The collection begun so many years ago when my baby hands reached through the bars of my playpen for a glittering object on the sands of Balboa Island had culminated in today's pair of perfect fan shells, held close to this grieving widow's heart.

I was shell struck.

Don't Cry Because It's Over, Smile Because It Happened

—Attributed to Dr. Seuss

March 2012. It is hard to imagine that Noel and I met only fourteen years ago. During our time together so many life-changing events happened to me— divorce, my parents' deaths, the marriages of my three children, breast cancer, and the births of six of my seven grandsons. I cannot imagine walking that journey alone without my best friend, Noel.

I have returned to Ireland to celebrate Heather's fortieth birthday. We will also gather the strands of Noel's, Mary's and my families for a reunion. Thirteen of us, my daughters and their families, Connie, my sister-in-law, Jenn, Heather's friend, and Walter and Lynne, Derek's father and stepmother, tumble off the plane at Cork Airport. Waiting for us in the Arrivals Hall are Noel's brother, Mick, Therese, their daughter, Gwen, and seven-year-old grandson Alex, all waving Irish flags in welcome. Suddenly I recall my first visit to meet Noel's family, when I had stepped uncertainly off the plane and run into the waiting arms of Noel. Now, as we stand in line at the Hertz Car Hire, I introduce everyone, while Alex and three of my grandsons kick a soccer ball around the airport lobby.

The next seventeen days at our Ballycotton home are a whirlwind of activity. Nancy, my first husband's sister and her family, Barry, Roberta (Barry's mother), and Brittany, arrive from the United States. On the first weekend, nearly everyone leaves for the St. Patrick's Day Festival in Dublin, while Connie and I remain with my grandsons to greet the friends and family who stop by for a chat. How do I explain the combinations of people who meet for the first time and quickly slip into easy conversation? At one point the sisters of Noel's first wife, Mary, and my sister-in-law from my first marriage sit together at the table while we play Uno. How Noel would have loved seeing everyone share a chat and a cup of tea! Our home in Ballycotton still welcomes, as it always will, our friends and family, the only requirement being to sign the guest book.

Whenever family gathers in Ballycotton they speak of feeling Noel's presence in the house and how they feel the warmth, love, and humor of his spirit. Because of Noel there is a full symphony of Irish names in my life—marvelous Gaelic names like Niamh and Aoife, Saorise and Kierse, and Sinead, and, of course, Dymphna and Betty—all wound up in the memories of our life together. Our American friends still recall Noel's Irish wit (his mighty *craic*), his quiet calming presence, and his ability to make each and every one of them feel special. They often tell me how much they miss him. Whenever I take one of Noel's roses, still blooming in my garden, to Betty Dooley, she breathes in the aroma. It reminds her of the after-church coffee chats we had over the years. She speaks of Noel as one of the nicest men she ever met and still laughs about how she had to listen to Mom's worries when we first met.

Noel's legacy lives on in his grandsons' memories. As I walk with the boys on Ballycotton's beaches, explore the harbor, and walk to the little store and post office in the village to buy candy, I speak of their Granda's heritage. They love to wear the Irish rugby and football jerseys I buy them. No, the boys have not forgotten their Granda. Johnathan and Austin let helium balloons fly to heaven for Granda on his birthday and on other days just to let him they are thinking of him...A year after Noel's death, Johnathan said,"Gramma, where is the candle snuffer? I have to teach Austin how Granda showed us to put out the candle!" During that difficult year, Grant once mentioned that Granda had died. Zach wanted to knew where he was, and Scott replied, "He is always with us." Declan said to me one day as we were driving. "I miss Granda. When will he come back?" In June 2011, as I was driving with Austin and Declan, they spotted an airplane. "I'm going to be a pilot," said Austin. "Where are you going to fly?" I asked. "I am going to go to heaven and bring Granda back to you."

"Oh, that would be great but you can't do that. He belongs in heaven now," I said tearfully.

"Oh, I will bring Jesus and God too," Austin said, with conviction.

That October, Zachary called me to tell me he no longer needed training wheels on his bike. "Wish I could have told Granda before he died," he quietly said.

So Noel remains present in their lives. Back in California, when we go off in the golf cart the boys ask me to go to the same places Noel took them, even though the adventure with their Granda looking for the alligator, the blue whales of the Dunes, rabbit hunting, rock beach, pelicans and secret bumps seemed more fun with him. In the way that he always pointed out birds and flowers to the boy, they now point out what they see to me. How fitting that the Granda Tree was dedicated in February 2011 at the Peter & Mary Muth Interpretative Center at Upper Newport Bay, where Noel spent so many hours sharing nature with the boys. All of his grandsons were at the dedication. With its sturdy trunk, long limbs, peacefulness, and life, this tree represents Noel as a man and as Granda. The boys took pictures in front of the tree, another of Noel's legacies.

The boys loved Noel's story times, especially his "Going on a Bear Hunt." Often they will ask me to read it. I don't have quite the inflection in my voice to scare them with "It's a BEAR!" but they remember well just how their Granda did it. Most importantly the boys remember their Granda's hugs. They hugged when they came in the house and when they left. Noel loved each and every one of his six grandsons. We were blessed again on December 27, 2010, by the birth of our seventh grandson, Brady Christopher Carey, his middle name in honor of Noel. Brady will grow up hearing the stories from his brothers and cousins of their remarkable Granda. And Noel's original signet ring? The leprechauns must have intervened there, too. Noel wore his ring until the day he died. It was later given to Brady on his first birthday.

I am still close to another who called Noel "Granda." Chrystal and Ben married in December of 2009. Before she began her walk down the aisle, I placed a tennis bracelet that Noel had given me on her wrist, so she could feel his presence that special day. She graduated in May of 2012 with an elementary education credential from Shepherdstown University, in Maryland. (Ben has his secondary education credential from the same university.) Their daughter, Emmalyn, was born on August 20, 2011. I once asked Chrystal whether she was just being nice in asking Noel to walk her down the aisle. She laughed and said, "Noel was a grandfather figure to me." She had had very few men in her life that did not let her down; Noel was one she knew she could always rely on.

> *I held him close for only a short time, but after he was gone, I'd see his smile on the face of a perfect stranger & I knew he would be there with me all the rest of my days.*
> **—Brian Andreas of the Story People**

During our reunion in Ireland, we also travel to the Ring of Kerry and explore the Dingle Peninsula, then spend a couple of nights in Killarney and continue to Shannon. It is one more bittersweet time, as Noel had loved this part of Ireland. July 1999 was the first of our trips to that area, and as the scenery sails past, I reflect on the memories we shared.

In Shannon we attend an afters party. (In Ireland it has become common for a bride and groom to host a late-night party for people not invited to the wedding or dinner).

This afters party was for Noel's nephew Paudie Scanlon and his wife Bebhine, at the Bunratty Manor Hotel. As we pass Bunratty Castle I experience deja vu, realizing that we had come full circle. This is where our families first met in January 2004. Now I am an Irish citizen. I, too, enjoy the mighty *craic.*

How do you end a love story? In a movie the characters fade from the screen. But in real life, or, shall I say, in my life, our love story continues. I live each day with Noel's memory, remembering our conversations, laughter, and love. I see him in the faces of perfect strangers as well as our friends. He taught us all to overlook people's shortcomings and to, as he would always say, "Give the guy a break." He taught us compassion for the human race and fought injustices in his quiet way.

Now at the afters party—what a fitting name—the outpouring of affection from my Irish family overwhelms me once again. And I think back to that lucky moment in Connemara when a man with twinkling blue eyes smiled at me, and said, "Hello, my name is Noel."

###

Acknowledgements

I want to thank my family, Heather, Derek, Jeff, Andrea, Wendy, Andy, and all of our seven grandsons, Scott, Grant, Johnathan, Declan, Zachary, Austin, and Brady, for being such a loving and supportive part of our story. Your total acceptance and love for Noel as stepdad and Granda was beyond my wildest dreams. We were a family, and each of you brought so much joy, happiness, and love to Noel and me that a simple thank you doesn't seem enough to express how you touched our hearts and souls, but thank you.

I also want to acknowledge the Cast of Characters you will find at the end of the book. Each of you shared our journey. We were blessed to have so many friends and family (from the Quinns to the McGraths, and the Beals to the Giulianos), all over the world, sharing moments of joy and sorrow and encouraging us to write our story. A special thank you goes to Yvette and Joan, who are like sisters to me. They were with Noel and me from the beginning, in Connemara, and watched our love grow. They, too, encouraged me in the writing of this book and, along with their husbands, Gary and Ken, shared wonderful moments and memories, Noel, Gary, and Ken could be called The Three Amigos.

Finally, last but definitely not least, I want to thank Jean Hastings Ardell, my memoir teacher and editor. Jean's entrance into my life was again an act of Irish magic. I had read in the Newport Beach Library Foundation "Bookmark" about a six-week memoir class offered by Jean in the spring of 2010. I thought this would be a perfect way for me to officially begin the writing of this book, but I set the notice aside and forgot about it. One day I ran into the library to return a book and literally ran into a sign that began to fall on me. As I righted the sign, I noticed that it announced the memoir class. This definitely caught my attention and I immediately signed up. Her teaching, information, and expertise inspired me to continue to write. She taught me to write it all down and edit later, which gave me the freedom to tell the story. She was the midwife for my story. Without her continued support and encouragement this book would still be in the process. I would write a chapter or so, send it over, and she would peruse it, edit it, and offer suggestions. And then, one day she told me that she had printed out the manuscript. I had written 150 pages. To say the least, I was flabbergasted. Again, a simple thank you is not enough. Noel would have loved your political passion, humor, enthusiasm for life, and your gift of gab. Thank you, Jeanie, for being my memoir teacher, editor, and friend. This story wouldn't have been written without you.

###

Cast of Characters
Noel Quinn

Family

Michael Quin (Noel's brother)
Therese Quin (sister in law)
    Graham Quin (Noel's nephew)
Nikki Quin (Graham's wife)

    Gary Quin (nephew)
    Wendy Quin (Gary's wife)

    Lelah Quin (great niece)
    Elliot Quin (great nephew)

    Gwen Quin (niece)
    Alex Quin (great nephew)

George Quinn (Noel's brother)
Kay Quinn (sister in law)
    Maria Nolen (niece & god daughter)
    Gerry McIntyre (partner)
        Jake Nolen (great nephew)
        Hayley Nolen (great niece)

    Pamela O'Brien (niece)
    Derek O'Brien (Pamela's husband)
        Evan O'Brien (great nephew)
        Ruby O'Brien (great niece)

    Phillip Quinn (nephew)
    Ruth Quinn (Phillip's wife
        Aoife Quinn (great niece)

Niamh Quinn (great niece)
Emmet Quinn (great nephew)
Aaron Quinn (great nephew)

Lilian Scanlon (sister)
Jerry Scanlon (brother in law)
    Sue Curley (niece)
    John Curley (Sue's husband)

    Tara Curley (niece)
        Saoirse Curley (great niece)
        Cillian Curley (great niece)
        Allanah Curley (great nephew)

    Georgie Curley (nephew)
    Alma Curley (Georgie's wife)
        Evin Curley (great nephew)
        Triona Curley (great niece)

    Tony Scanlon (nephew)
    Miriam Scanlon
        Rachel Scanlon (great niece)

    Paul Scanlon (nephew)
    Ann Scanlon (Paul's wife)
        Keava Scanlon (great niece)
        Niamh Scanlon (great niece)

Greg Scanlon (nephew)
Jean Scanlon (Greg's wife)
   David Scanlon (great nephew)
   Sinead Scanlon (David's wife)
      Fionn Scanlon (great nephew)
      Sadhbh Scanlon (great niece)
      Cormac Scanlon (great nephew)
   Paudie Scanlon (great nephew)
   Bebhine Scanlon (wife of Paudie)
   Julie Scanlon (great niece)

Mella Malone (niece)
Ollie Malone (Mella's husband)
   Shane Malone (great nephew)
   Ian Malone (great nephew)

Dervalanne Kilvane (niece)
Tony Kilvane (husband of Dervalanne)
   Lisa Kilvane (great niece)
   Jamie Kilvane (great nephew)
   Ellie Kilvane (great niece)

Robbie Scanlon (nephew)
Amanda Hussey (Robbie's partner)

American Friends

Joan Bovard
Ken Bovard
   Darren Bovard
   Danielle Bovard
   Jarrod Bovard
   Christina Bovard

Yvette Kilgore
Gary Kilgore
   Lori Benfield (daughter)
   Steve Benfield
      Garrett Benfield
   Jacob Kilgore (son)
   Liam Kilgore
   Jason Kilgore (son)
   Lisa Kilgore
      Jordan Kilgore
      Jonah Kilgore
Betty Dooley

Penny Popov (Betty's daughter)
Jim Popov
Pat Brown (Betty's daughter)
Jon Brown
Pam Rybus (Betty's daughter)
Tom Rybus
Margie Beal
Tom Beal

Debbie Mason
Bill Mason
Rita Bishop
Larry Bishop
Mike Brenna
Henri Moscaro
Faye Diedtker
Don Diedtker
Terrie Klein
   Chrystal Klein Copenhaver
   Ben Copenhaver
   Emmalyn Copenhaver

Carol Westling
Jim Westling
Delores Hall (Andrea's Mom)
Wayne Hall (Andrea's Dad)
Jeff Hall (Andrea's brother)
Susan Carey (Andy's Mom)
Dave Carey (Andy's Dad)
Nick Carey (Andy's brother)
April Carey (Andy's sister in law)
Page Weddle (Derek's Mom)
Walter Anderson (Derek's Dad)
Lynne Anderson (Derek's step-mom)
Jenn Ruben
Julia Ratcliffe (English Rotary Exchange Daughter)
Lori Brower
Jimmy Brower
    Brendon Brower
    Brooke Brower
Marcella Reyes and Family
Dr. Vandermolen (Ann & Noel's oncologist)

Dr. Patrick Pan (internist)
Claudia Thomas
Teri McKesson
Mike McKesson
Wendy Bennett
Mike Bennett
P. L. Domingo
Lindsey Deems
Kris Duncan
Kirk Duncan
Tamara O'Donnell
Aumee Frey
Jason Frey
Paul Niday
Kevin Moore
Marisa Simone
Candi Anderson
Vivian Rodriguez
Willard Reisz (attorney)
Steve Norin (stock advisor)
Beverle Chenault
Jerry Davis
Gloria Hanson (cruise tour)

The McGrath Family
(Noel's first wife, Mary)

Mrs. Mary McGrath (Noel's Mother in law, Mary's Mum)

Sean McGrath (Mary's brother and owner of McGrath's Pub in Ballycotton)
Denise McGrath (Sean's wife)
    Michael McGrath (nephew)
    Liz McGrath (Michael's wife)
        Thomas McGrath (great nephew)
        Emma McGrath (great niece)

Paul McGrath (nephew who lives in Sydney)
Jenny McGrath (Paul's wife)
    Alex McGrath (great nephew)
    Madeleine McGrath (great niece)

John McGrath (nephew)

Jean McGrath (niece)
    Leah McGrath (great niece)

Susan McGrath (niece)
Denis Lyne (Susan's partner)

Margaret "Mags" McGrath (niece)

Phil McGrath (Mary's brother)
Kay McGrath (Phil's wife)

Monsignor Tom McGrath (Mary's brother in England)

Niamh O'Connor (niece)
Rich O'Connor (Niamh's husband)
    David O'Connor (great nephew)
    Anna O'Connor (great niece)
    Sarah O'Connor (great nephew)

Betty (Sister Eilish) McGrath (Mary's sister and Catholic nun)

Michael McGrath (Mary's brother)
Sheila McGrath (Michaels's wife)
    Michelle Murphy (niece)
    Noel Murphy (Michelle's husband)
        Micheal Murphy (great nephew)

Sean McGrath (nephew)
Connor McGrath (nephew)

Dymphna Crowe (Mary's sister)
Eddie Crowe (Dymphna's husband)
    Stephen Crowe (nephew)
    Melanie Crowe (Stephen's wife)
        Theodore "Theo" Crowe (great nephew)

Marie Hicks (niece)
Tom Hicks (Marie's husband)

Tom McGrath (nephew)
Maria McGrath (Tom's wife)
    Clara McGrath (great niece)

Micheal McGrath (nephew)

Kieran Crowe (nephew)

Annie Quinn

Family

Marge Stonebraker (Annie's Mom)
John Stonebraker (Annie's Dad)

Heather Anderson (Annie's daughter)
Derek Anderson (son in law)
    Declan Anderson (grandson, b. 2007)

Jeffrey Giuliano (Annie's son)
Andrea Giuliano (daughter in law)
    Scott Giuliano (grandson 2002)
    Grant Giuliano (grandson 2004)
    Zachary Giuliano (grandson 2007)

Wendy Carey (Annie's daughter)
Andrew (Andy) Carey (son in law)

Johnathan Carey (grandson 2004)
Austin Carey (grandson 2007)
Brady Carey (grandson 2010)

Dodie Bollard (Annie's aunt)
Boyd Bollard (Uncle)
    Susie McCormick (Cousin)
    Eric McCormick
    Erin McCormick
    Kristen McCormick

    Bob Bollard (cousin)
    Juanita Bollard (Bob's wife)

Lynda Pond (Annie's sister)
Lenard Pond (Lynda's husband)

Sherry Sourapas (niece)
David Sourapas (Sherry's husband)
    Ashley Sourapas (great niece)
    Amanda Sourapas (great niece)
    Tyler Sourapas (great nephew)

Michael Pond (nephew)
Yolanda Pond (Michael's wife)
    Bryanne Pond (great niece)
    Ryan Pond (great nephew)

Irish Friends

Ann Warren
Bob Warren
Mark Warren (Noel's godson)
Holly Warren (Mark's wife)
Claire Warren
Paul Warren
Dr. Maura Cohr Kelly
Don Kelly
Father Mick Waters (Catholic priest/Denise McGrath's brother)

Eileen Cotter
Carmel Murphy
Michael Murphy
Jo Twoomey
Mary Barrett
John Barrett
John Brown
Reverend Desmond Doyle
Martin Tattan
Father Donal O'Brien
Father John O'Brien

The Giuliano Family
(Annie's first husband, Jim)

Jim Giuliano (ex-husband)

Salvatore Giuliano (Annie's father in law)

Paula Boelts (Annie's sister in law)
Tom Boelts (Paula's husband)
Tommy Boelts (nephew)
Theresa Boelts (Tom's wife)
Hunter Boelts (great nephew)
Tommy Boelts (great nephew)
Maggie Boelts (great nephew)
Shelby (great niece)
Danielle (great niece)
Dustin (great nephew)

Tammy Wade (niece)
Steve Wade (husband of Tammy)
Joel Wade (great nephew)
Josh Wade (great nephew)
Jesse Wade (great nephew)
Giuliana Wade (great niece)

Nancy Fisher (sister in law)
Barry Fisher (Nancy's husband)
Ryan Fisher (nephew)
Margaret Fisher (Ryan's wife)

Justyn Fisher (great nephew)
Jayden Fisher (great nephew)
Jessyca Fisher (great niece)

Jason Fisher (nephew)
Kelly Fisher (Jason's wife)
Ava Fisher (great niece)
Ella Fisher (great niece)

Tiffany Hudson (niece)
Robert Hudson (Tiffany's husband)
Tanner Hudson (great nephew)
Fisher Hudson (great nephew)

Brittany Fisher (niece)
Jordan Fisher (nephew)

Roberta Fisher (Barry's Mom)
Oliver Fisher (Barry's Dad)
Brenda Newton (Barry's sister)
Frank Newton (Brenda's husband)
Ashley Newton
Nicholas Newton

Connie Maguinness (sister in law)
Bob Maguinness (Connie's husband)
Kellie Maguinness (niece)
Matthew Maguinness (nephew)

Adam Maguinness
(nephew)
Josh Maguinness
(nephew)
Amy Maguinness (Josh's
wife)
Jackson Maguinness
(great nephew)
Carter Maguinness
(great nephew)

Susan Giuliano
John Giuliano (Jim's cousin)

Pauline Lynn (Jim's cousin)
Jim Lynn

Barbara Giuliano McMurray
(Jim's cousin)
Sean McMurray

A word about *A Word with You Press*
Publishers and Purveyors of Fine Stories

In addition to being a full service publishing house, *A Word with You Press* is a playful, passionate and prolific consortium of writers connected by our collective love of the written word. We are, as well, devoted readers, drawn to the notion that there is nothing more beautiful or powerful than a well-told story.

www.awordwithyoupress.com is the planet we inhabit in cyberspace, although writers lucky enough to live in the San Diego area are also welcome at our clubhouse headquarters in Oceanside, California, at 802 South Tremont Street. We offer multiple posts and columns, created exclusively for our readers. Read Ed Coonce's *Musings from East Hell Blvd.*, get a British flavored giggle from Ruth Joyce's serial cartoon *Wuss'n'Boots*, and raise the curtain on your own ambitions with Theresa Ann Brassington's interactive *Let's Make a Scene* for aspiring screen writers. Our most frequently visited feature remains our monthly writing competition to encourage and inspire writers to stretch their imaginations without stretching a deadline.

We realize that great writers and artists don't just happen. They are nurtured, inspired and mentored. They are the lucky few who discover that art is not a diversion or distraction from everyday life; rather, art is an essential expression of the human spirit. *A Word with You Press* is so profoundly committed to this belief that we have founded a non-profit organization, *Kid Expression,* to provide free mentoring to children to help them find their inner artists, and give them the tools to express themselves beautifully through the written word.

Our *Kid Expression* workshop, led by volunteer mentors, combines one-on-one instruction with group activities. To honor their accomplishments, each child who completes the workshop is rewarded with a debut book-signing event, where they can see their own work in print as part of an anthology published by *A Word with You Press*. Visit www.kidexpression.org, a 501 (c) 3 not-for-profit organization to learn more, donate, or investigate how you could sponsor a satellite in your literary community.

From the desk of
Editor-in-Chief
Thornton Sully

Do you have a literary project that you'd like to discuss?

We offer a full range of publishing services, including editing, book and cover design, and marketing. We have published A Pulitzer Prize winner, an award winning poet, a literary anthology, a young adult book, a couple's guide, personal memoirs, mainstream fiction and even *The One Minute Bartender.*

Recently we have achieved international status, with distribution for selected titles in Europe.

Let us help you with our project. We'll be happy to give you a pro-bono evaluation of the first thirty pages of your work, and see if it is something we might work upon together to make public.

Send your inquiries to info@awordwithyoupress.com as a separate word attachment. Show us what you've got.

Best regards,

Thornton Sully
Editor-in-Chief
A Word with You Press

CPSIA information can be obtained at www.ICGtesting.com
Printed in the USA
BVOW010017180213

313452BV00001B/1/P